The Little Book of

DREAM
SYMBOLS

Asta – good dreams
May all your ∨ dreams
come true! Happy
Easter 2017. Love
you always –
Mom & Dad

The Little Book of
DREAM
SYMBOLS

The Essential Guide to Over 700
of the Most Common Dreams

JACQUELINE TOWERS

HAMPTON ROADS

Cover design by Jim Warner
Cover illustration © Natalia Moroz / istock
Interior design by Kathryn Sky-Peck

Hampton Roads Publishing Company, Inc.
Charlottesville, VA 22906
Distributed by Red Wheel/Weiser, LLC
www.redwheelweiser.com
Sign up for our newsletter and special offers by going to
www.redwheelweiser.com/newsletter/

ISBN: 978-1-57174-758-7
Library of Congress Control Number: 2016956361

Printed in the United States of America
M&G
10 9 8 7 6 5 4 3 2 1

Contents

An Introduction to Dreams

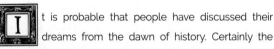 t is probable that people have discussed their dreams from the dawn of history. Certainly the Bible and other early texts contain stories about important or prophetic dreams, with the most famous being Joseph's dreams of a famine in Egypt and Jacob's dream of a ladder leading to heaven. Every race and culture in the world tells stories about dreams, and dream books are not confined to the Western world. Such books have existed for centuries in the Middle and Far East, and especially in Iran, where dreams are considered important indicators of future events.

Lucid dreaming means choosing the dream you want to have and concentrating on it before falling asleep. The purpose is to allow your mind to work on the subject contained in the dream and maybe even transmit it to another person. If you can do this, the dream will take place not soon after falling asleep but an hour or two before waking. Some people can do this; others cannot.

Eugene Aserinsky and Nathaniel Kleitman discovered REM (rapid eye movement) sleep in 1953. Their research has shown us that dreams occur during set ninety-minute periods when the eyes appear to move about and muscles twitch and move. Those who swear that they never dream just do not remember their dreams. Fortunately, most people do remember some of their dreams.

Sigmund Freud and Carl Gustav Jung are the founders of modern psychoanalysis and are the first medical men to take dreams seriously, concluding that they tell a lot about the state of a patient's mind. Jung suggested to his patients that if they surface during the night with a vivid dream in mind, they should write it down right away, because it is difficult to recall the dream later.

Today, there are conflicting arguments about the importance of dreams, because some people consider that every dream you remember tells you something about your state of mind. Some people believe that dreams are prophetic, and yet other people consider that dreams are nothing more than the mind's way of clearing space for the new information that will shortly be coming its way. In my experience as a psychic counselor and medium, I believe all these things. Some dreams do seem to be a way of clearing space in the mind, while others show how we feel at any point in time, but there are definitely also prophetic dreams.

Sometimes a relative who has died will visit a sleeping person and bring a message. It is often easier for this person

the little book of dream symbols

to get through to a loved one in this way, so any messages of this type can contain useful advice or a warning. Some dreams foretell the future by showing the dreamer exactly what is due to happen, but most do so symbolically. The human mind resonates with certain symbols, and a book like this will help you to discover what these symbols mean. Sometimes two people have an almost identical dream; such dreams are usually prophetic.

The rather weird idea of opposite or contrary dreams is an old one. These are dreams that seem to predict good events but actually predict bad ones, and vice versa. So now, use this dream dictionary to untangle the meaning behind your dreams, and then use the advice or warning that dreams bring you to your advantage.

As you begin interpreting your dreams, consider the images that the dreams are giving you. Consider sayings such as "Go with the flow," "Where there's smoke, there's fire," "You can't see the forest for the trees," "It never rains, but it pours," and so on. If a certain image means something to you, check the interpretation in this book, but also go with your own feeling about the image. For instance, a wheel could indicate travel to one person, the passage of time to another, and a roulette wheel and the wheel of fortune to someone else.

Nightmares

Nightmares can be nature's way of allowing us to express thoughts and feelings that we either push away during the day or that are bothering us more than we realize. Some nightmares are of the chasing variety, in which we cannot reach our destination, while others are of chasing after something that is getting away from us. Both these types of dreams show us that our lives are overloaded with stress and responsibilities.

Sometimes nightmares are the mind's way of coping with severe trauma after a frightening experience or after a period of severe danger. A friend of mine had nightmares every night for about six weeks after being in a car accident. Also, those who survive war situations may especially be beset by occasional nightmares for the rest of their lives. In fact, the word "trauma" comes from the German, *traum*, which means dream.

Many times nightmares intrude into our waking lives and disturb us, which means that they are alerting us to something—good or bad—to come. Alternatively, a nightmare may be a form of warning that can alert you to a problem in your normal waking life, especially if it is a recurring nightmare. For instance, a friend of mine kept having dreams about choking, which she interpreted as a message that she should quit smoking. She stopped smoking and the nightmares quickly stopped. In this case, her body was sending her messages via her subconscious.

Here is another strange story. A friend of mine used to dream about crossing a rope bridge, similar to the ones you see in adventure films that span a gorge with a fast-flowing river below. In the dream, my friend was a primitive native person. She crossed the swaying bridge while holding her small daughter by the hand. The daughter lost her footing and slipped off the bridge, but my friend managed to haul her back by hand. They both survived the crossing, but her daughter's arm was broken. The odd thing is that her daughter used to have the same recurring dream, except that she was the child holding on to her mother's hand in the dream. While my friend's daughter was playing on a swing set in a neighbor's garden one day, she fell and broke her arm badly. Was this dream a reference to a previous life? Was it a warning to the child not to climb? Was it just a strange coincidence? We'll never know.

DREAM
SYMBOLS

 through

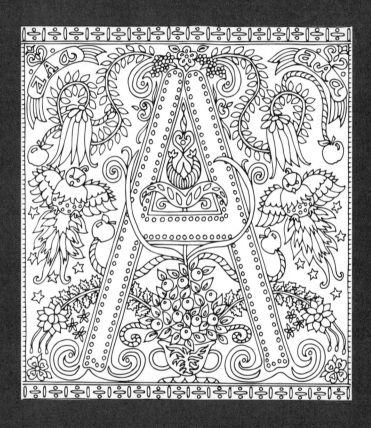

Abandonment   This can be a contrary dream. If you dream that someone abandons you, it actually means that you will reunite with a lover or old friend. On the other hand, if you dream of abandoning someone else, then this dream warns that you could lose that person. Abandoning something in your dream is actually lucky, and you could have good luck with money.

Abroad   If you dream that you are in a different country, it means that things around you are unsettled and that you may be moving. A new and influential friend is on the way if you dream of traveling abroad by ship.

Abyss   This is a good dream to have so long as you do not fall into the abyss. It indicates that you will overcome any obstacles or difficulties. If, however, you dream that you fall in, then the dream indicates that you should be extremely careful in all of your business dealings.

Accident   To dream of an accident means exactly what you think it means: it is a warning of an impending accident. Therefore, if you are planning to travel, it may be best to delay your trip for a day or two. If you dream of having an accident at sea, this relates to a love affair and emotional issues. However, if you dream of the accident on land, this relates to business affairs. If the dream involves accidents of another nature, such as sharp instruments, electricity, fire, and the like, then you are advised to avoid these things over the next few days.

Accounts/Accountants   As you would expect, this is a dream about money. If you dream about adding up your accounts, it is a warning not to lend money. If your figures balance perfectly, it means a profitable proposition is coming your way. If you dream of balancing the accounts at work, it is a warning to be careful of your enemies.

Ace   Each suit has its own meaning. Hearts bring success in love and wishes coming true. Diamonds denote that you will have good luck in money. Clubs mean that you will be successful despite quarrels in business matters. Spades equates to sadness and little reward for your work efforts. If you are unaware of the particular suit, this suggests an unsolved mystery.

the little book of dream symbols

Acorn This is an immensely lucky dream. Dreaming of acorns foretells the successful outcome of any problems you may be experiencing, and prosperity and good fortune for the future—from little acorns great oak trees grow.

Acrobat If you dream of an acrobat performing, this dream warns you not to take any journeys for at least a week. If you dream of yourself as the performing acrobat, you will overcome current difficulties faster than you expected. If you see someone you know as the acrobat, it is a warning to look out for deception by that person. Dreaming of an acrobat falling or having an accident indicates that you will actually have a lucky escape from danger.

Adultery Dreaming of adultery indicates problems in your love life that are causing you great concern. It is a warning that you should not confide your fears to new friends, as they will betray your confidence. If you take heed of this warning, then any setbacks will only be temporary. If you dream of your wife committing adultery, then expect arguments with your neighbors. If you dream of your husband committing adultery, then you could be in for an inheritance.

Airplane   If you see an airplane taking off in your dream, success is on the way, but if you see it landing, you should be careful of jealous friends. If you see just yourself traveling in an airplane, you will experience some reversals in your life, especially if the weather in your dream is bad. If you see the airplane crash, as expected it signifies a major failure. Contrary to the dream, if you see yourself in a disaster, this indicates financial gain. If you see yourself being killed in a crash, all it means is that you must control your passions.

Alcohol   If you see yourself just having a moderate social drink, then success is indicated. However, if you see yourself drinking to excess, you may have to make an embarrassing apology.

Alley   Seeing, or being in, a dark alley is a warning that people close by are talking about you. However, if the alley is bright and clear, then your road ahead is equally clear. If you see an alley with a dead end, the dream warns that you should think carefully before embarking on any action.

Alligator   Seeing an alligator warns that you must be very wary of other people or a new project, as this could affect your life dramatically. Treachery and secret enemies are about.

Almond   Expect some temporary sorrow. If you dreamed that you ate the nuts, you will have luck if you enjoyed them, but if they tasted bitter, it is a warning to delay decision-making. To see an almond tree in full bloom indicates happy celebrations in the home.

Altar   This suggests that you will soon be released from your worries and that good news from an unexpected source is about to be received.

Ambulance   This dream is a warning about being indiscreet with the opposite sex, because if you are outspoken you will suffer repercussions. A full ambulance suggests that you will achieve your hopes sooner than you think. If the ambulance is empty, be warned that you will lose a close friend. Financial difficulties could soon be experienced if you see yourself calling for an ambulance for relatives, but if you call one for yourself, then an illness will soon be over.

Amorousness   To feel yourself being amorous in a dream suggests that an exciting romance is about to blossom. If someone else is being amorous toward you, a relationship could cause extreme embarrassment or even scandal.

Anchor   This is a warning to economize for a few months.

Angel   This is a wonderful dream to have, as seeing one or more angels foretells success, protection, happiness, and rewarding friendships in your life.

Anger   This is a contrary dream. If your anger is directed toward someone else, it indicates that you will gain material benefit through a friend. If the object or person is unknown to you, you will soon celebrate. If you dream of being verbally abused, it is a warning about business.

Ants   Seeing ants in the home warns of illness in the family. Watching ants at work indicates success through perseverance, although you will have some difficulties to overcome in the early stages. Ants crawling over food are a good omen that predicts happiness. Some dream interpreters suggest that dreaming of ants denotes problems with one's mother-in-law!

Anvil   To see yourself or someone purchasing an anvil signifies spectacular luck is on the way and—providing there is no noise—happiness is assured. However, if the noise is loud, then you can expect a quick change of location.

Apartment   If the apartment in your dream is uncomfortable and small, you will have to be patient. If the apartment is large and well decorated, there will be a steady increase in your prosperity.

Ape   This warns you to beware of enemies in your business or social circle that are being underhanded and making mischief. You also need to pay more attention to your work.

Apology   This dream relates to friends, whether the apology is given or received. You may gain a new friend, lose an existing one, or be pleasantly surprised by the return of an old one.

Apples   If you are eating a ripe, sweet apple in your dream, this is a good omen. It brings happiness and the promise of well-earned rewards, and it signals a new love entering your life, inciting temptation. If the apple is unripe and bitter, it is a warning that you could lose much through your own foolishness.

Arch   If the arch is whole, your efforts are heading in the right direction and benefits can be expected or a fresh start can be made. If the arch is damaged, it is an indication to reexamine situations and make the necessary changes.

Archer   If you are single, seeing an archer in your dream indicates that you will soon find the right partner. Should you be married, however, it is a warning to resist temptation.

Arguments   This is a contrary dream. Any form of argument in your dream signals a resolution of disputes. However, should you lose your temper while arguing, this is a warning that you should think before you act and guard against making impulsive decisions.

Arm   An injured arm signals a warning that you should have a medical checkup.

Arrest   If you see yourself arrested, expect a severe disappointment that is quickly followed by an unexpected joyous occasion. If you are set free, sudden success will come to you. You can expect a surprise gift if you see someone else arrested in your dream.

Artist   If you are the artist, you will need to reconsider your plans in order to achieve the recognition you are looking for. If you see an artist, it is a warning that you are wasting your time on frivolous activities.

Assault   If you dream of being assaulted, someone will pass on some very important information to you. If you see others being assaulted, you may have to defend an attack on your character. If you assault others, money could be on its way to you.

Audience   If you face an audience, then you can expect a surprising accolade to come your way. If you are in the audience, then you can find yourself celebrating with a friend over his or her good fortune.

Author   Do not lend any money if you see an author at work in your dream, as this is an indication that your finances will be strained in the near future.

Avalanche   You should think about changing your plans. If you are buried in an avalanche, you can expect an incredible stroke of good luck. If you see others buried in an avalanche, this indicates a change of address.

Ax   If the ax is bright and clean, you can expect the rewards for work that you have done well. If the ax is dull and dirty, then you may experience a loss of prestige that could have been avoided had you paid closer attention to your business affairs.

Baby Dreaming of a pretty baby or babies means that you will benefit from the help of friends. If the baby or babies are ugly, then take it as a warning that someone you trust is being deceitful—ugly baby, ugly friend! You need to be cautious in your business and love affairs if you see sick or helpless babies. To see a walking baby foretells of sudden independence. If you see many babies in your dream, you can expect enormous satisfaction and happiness to come your way.

Bag If the bag is made of paper and is empty, it is a warning to be more cautious in your dealings—paper is not secure. You can expect business success when you dream of a cloth bag. A leather bag indicates unexpected but delightful travel. Heavy or full bags are particularly lucky.

Balcony This is an obstacle dream. If the balcony seems dangerous, or has collapsed, then expect to hear some sad news from distant friends.

Ball Playing any ball games means happy news is on its way. If you see a masquerade ball, this is a warning against friends who are not being honest.

the little book of dream symbols

Ballet When a woman dreams of ballet, it is a warning to her to keep a watchful eye on her partner, who might wish to dance a pas de deux with someone else. For a man, it is a warning to be very careful of his business affairs, as failure is strongly indicated.

Banana If you eat a banana, expect a period of hard work coming but with very little reward—bananas take three hours to digest! If the banana is damaged in any way, friends will disappoint you.

Bank If you see an empty bank, losses will be suffered. If you are depositing or receiving money, you can expect some luck in money matters. To see cashiers paying money out is a warning not to be careless in financial matters.

Bar Dreaming of tending a bar indicates that you will resort to some controversial actions. If you are only drinking or just observing what is going on in a bar, then it is time you interested yourself in the affairs of the community.

Barn A full barn denotes prosperity; an empty or derelict one warns against making risky investments.

Baseball   A happy home life is promised, especially if you win the game. You can also expect to receive help from family and friends.

Bat   If the bat frightens you, you should not discuss your affairs, because there is deception around you. If you are not frightened, you can look forward to being offered a profitable proposition.

Bathing   To dream of bathing in the open sea indicates that you will receive a fortune beyond your wildest dreams. Bathing in a river also predicts a pleasant surprise. To see yourself bathing in a lake indicates that you will have trouble but it will pass. Bathing with other people means that a friend will approach you for help.

Bathtub   If the bathtub is empty, this is a warning to you not to carry out decisions or actions when you are angry. If the bath feels too hot or too cold, revise a plan that you are enthusiastic about. If the bath is warm and pleasant, it is an indication that your current expectations will be realized.

Beach   This is a contrary dream. If you see yourself lazing on a beach, expect to be incredibly busy with a new venture. If you dream of working on a beach, this means that you will soon be likely to need financial help.

Beans   Dreaming of beans indicates that there are difficulties ahead—rather like Jack and the Beanstalk. If you see the beans being cooked, then smile, because it signifies an increase in your income.

Bear   Killing or fighting off a bear in your dream suggests victory over a hostile situation around you. A caged bear indicates success in the future. To see a dancing bear suggests that you will receive luck in anything speculative.

Bed   To be in your own bed is a promise of security. If you find yourself in a strange bed, it is a sign that there will be an upturn in your business dealings. If you are making a bed, you can expect visitors.

Beer   This is a good omen if you see yourself drinking or pouring beer, particularly if it had a nice frothy head on it. If the beer is flat and unpalatable, it is a stern warning that you should not be involved in intrigue that could backfire on you and damage your reputation.

Bees   These industrious insects are the forerunner of good fortune in business matters, even if you see yourself being stung by them. However, if you kill them or see them dead or listless, you could suffer loss by putting too much trust in those you consider friends. To hear bees buzzing in your dream indicates that good news is on its way.

Beetles   Dreaming of beetles is a warning to you that there is jealousy, and even hostility, among your colleagues. If you succeed in killing them or getting rid of them, then the difficulties will only be temporary.

Beggar   When you see a beggar or help one, you will receive some unexpected help. If you refuse a beggar, someone you rely on will let you down.

Bell   To hear a single bell of any kind in your dream indicates that you will receive rather disappointing news. If you hear the noise of several bells, expect to hear some happy news. Church bells warn that people are working against you.

Bereavement   This is an opposite dream. Happy news is on its way, and this news may be about a birth, an engagement, or a wedding.

Bicycle   Take note of whether you are pushing the bike uphill, riding downhill, or riding on the flat, as this will show whether your future will be tough, easy, or as things are now.

Bills   This is a contrary dream. There will be a lucky period in financial matters if you dream of receiving bills or you are worrying about them. You will need help shortly if you see yourself paying or sending out bills.

Birds   This is a lucky dream, especially if the birds are brightly colored, singing, or flying. Injured birds warn that worries are on their way. If you see a bird of prey, your worries will be short-lived. To see birds' eggs in a nest indicates money, but broken eggs denote disappointments. To see birds hatching out of the eggs tells of delayed profits. If you see an empty nest in your dream, do not allow yourself to be drawn into family arguments.

Birth   Dreaming of giving birth is a strong indication that you will soon be the recipient of good news. A multiple birth is an indication of material wealth. To dream of animals giving birth tells that anyone who may be scheming and working against you will soon be defeated in their efforts.

Blackmail   If you dream that you are being black-mailed, give up any indiscreet conduct with the opposite sex. If you see yourself as the blackmailer, this is definitely not the time for you to gamble.

Blame   This is a contrary dream. If you see yourself being blamed, do not worry, as it indicates that you will have unusual luck in business. If the blame is attached to other people, take it as a warning that there is deception around you.

Blanket   Guard your investments well if someone gives you blankets or if you purchase them. If you are poor in your dream, you can expect some financial gain. Blankets that are in a poor condition show deception from a friend.

Blemish   If the blemish is on the neck, chest, bust, or arms, then you are in for a hot time with the opposite sex. Beware if the blemish is on the body or legs, as you will be embroiled in a dangerous scandal.

Blood   This is a time of hard work for you against strong opposition. If you are bleeding, you must guard against getting into arguments with family or friends.

Blossom   This tells you that you will be better off by next spring. If it is spring at the time of the dream, a better life is on the way.

Boat   This foretells a journey that is connected with love or romance. If the sea is very stormy, there may be trouble in the near future in connection with love.

Bomb   All dreams of weapons and explosives foretell danger and trouble, so be prepared for a bumpy ride ahead.

Book If your children are reading books, a happy and harmonious time is in store for your family. If you are reading, you need begin to research something or embark on a course of study.

Bookcase If the bookcase is filled with books, you can look forward to a good career. If it is empty, you will find your job boring and irritating.

Boomerang A boomerang means that you have lost someone or something, but they will soon come back to you. It also means that any good or bad deeds that you have done will come back to you.

Box If the box is full, you can expect a windfall, but if it is empty, you will be short of money for a while.

Bracelet If the bracelet is not broken, it symbolizes union and partnership, which can indicate the start of a phase. If the bracelet is broken, it means that a partnership is at an end.

Brandy Brandy suggests that you want to be a social success in a stratum of society.

Bread   Bread means good luck and prosperity is on the way, but it won't come without hard work. Don't do things for your children that are not necessary, as they will take everything you have to give and be extremely ungrateful in return.

Breakfast   Seeing breakfast on a table and eating it with others is a good omen, but it can denote that a period of change is on the way. Eating alone is not a good omen, as it suggests that you have enemies who might get the better of you.

Bribe   If you give or receive bribes you will be caught.

Bride, Bridegroom, Bridesmaid   Dreams of weddings and the people who are at the heart of them are always a symbol of disappointment in love. If you want to marry a certain man, think twice before rushing into doing so. The best aspect of this dream is that it can mean that a legacy is coming your way.

Bridge   If the bridge is complete and you can cross it safely, the end of a period of trouble is near. If the bridge is broken or if you have an accident while crossing it, you must consider your future path because what you want to do doesn't look secure. If you pass under a bridge, there will be a temporary period of uncertainty.

Briefcase This is a contrary dream because it is best if the briefcase is empty, as this means improvements in business. If it is full, you will be faced with losses.

Broadcast Hearing a broadcast or making one can indicate a spell of sickness or a disappointment.

Broom This is a straightforward dream, as it means that you will clear up things that are still hanging around and make a fresh start with a "new broom."

Brother If the brother in the dream is doing well, you will be all right too, but if he is poor and unhappy, you may be in for a bad spell yourself.

Brush Dreaming of brushing your hair is a bad omen, as it means misfortune, mismanagement, and muddles, but dreaming of brushing clothes indicates that your hard work will pay off in the long run.

A number of brushes suggest that you will soon have a variety of jobs to do rather than one single one.

Buckle   A buckle that is fastened brings happiness in family life, but one that is unfastened suggests arguments and trouble in the family. If you find yourself fastening a buckle, you must pay attention to business affairs.

Bubbles   You can expect to attend or throw a party, and either way, you will have a lot of fun!

Bugle   Hearing or seeing a bugle means that good news and happy times are on the way.

Building   If you are working on a building, you are laying the foundations for something that will last and you are building a new and better future for yourself. A newly completed building means your plans are about to come into being.

Bull   Someone who was born under the sign of Taurus will soon be important to you, but your new friend may be stubborn.

Bulldog   A friendly dog is a sign of success. If the dog is unfriendly, you must be sure to be honest and lawful at all times.

Burden   This is an obvious dream. If you are carrying a burden, you are probably weighed down in real life. If you put the burden down, you will soon be feeling less burdened in your waking life.

Burial   This has nothing to do with death or burials, as it denotes a windfall and a happy marriage or partnership. If you dream that someone else is being buried, it means that this person will soon travel or move away.

Burn   Dreaming of burning or being burned is an omen of success and an end to your present troubles. It indicates good friends and good fortune to come.

Bus   Waiting for a bus suggests that it will take time for you to achieve your ambition, but if you get on the bus in the dream, you will get what you want pretty quickly. An accident denotes money worries.

the little book of dream symbols

Butcher   This is a bad omen all around. Watching a butcher killing an animal is a warning of sickness for you or your family. Seeing meat being cut up is a warning to watch what you say, to take care in what you put in writing, and not to bother to ask for a character reference, as you will not get a good one.

Butter   Butter has always represented abundance, so it denotes good health and success. If you sell butter in your dream, it means small gains and windfalls.

Butterfly   This shows prosperity and success as long as you can stick to what you are doing. A number of butterflies mean great news from family and friends, while a lone butterfly can also mean success and happiness in love. This is clearly a good omen all around.

Button   This brings happiness and wealth in marriage to a woman dreamer. If the dreamer is male, it denotes a good future career.

Buzzard   A buzzard means someone will try to take what you have and there will be arguments, losses, scandal, and gossip.

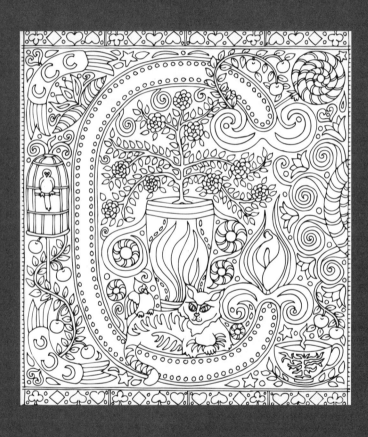

Cabin   If the cabin is situated within woods or on a beach, then family happiness is assured. If you see a ship's cabin, it warns of a stormy time ahead in both family and business matters. A legal battle could ensue concerning a friend or colleague.

Cage   To see a full cage of birds signifies a sizable inheritance that will relieve you from any anxieties that you may have. An empty cage is a warning for you to not be careless and to beware of missing a good opportunity. If you see two birds in a cage, it means success in love.

Cake   This is a lucky dream. You will be successful in all aspects of your life concerning social and business matters, particularly if you see yourself eating the cake. If the cake is very sweet, then expect a promotion at work or a financial gift to come your way. If the cake is covered in thick icing, you can be sure of some happy times ahead.

Camp   A summer or holiday camp signifies a change in your workplace or the place where you live. If it is a military camp, it signals success in a business venture.

Cancer   This is a contrary dream. You can look for-ward to a long life on the provision that you remem-ber not to overindulge yourself in all areas.

Candle   To see lighted candles is a happy promise that things are going to improve in all areas of your life. However, if the candles are unlit, disappoint-ments are in store concerning your love life. Short candles imply that new opportunities will be open-ing up for you. If you see candlesticks being carried, you can look forward to an increase in your social life.

Canyon   This portends quarrels and disagreements over finance, particularly if the canyon is lined with trees. It is a warning that you should avoid any dis-cussions of this nature over the next few days.

Cap   This is a great dream to have if you see your-self wearing a cap. It is a good sign that any problems you may be experiencing will only be temporary ones. If the cap is old, worn out, or in poor condition, you can expect some slight setbacks in any business dealings. If the cap is of a military type, this foretells of victory in spite of serious resistance.

Captive   This type of dreams warns of worry and tension due to financial matters that have been stretched through overspending. If you see animals that are captive, this shows that life is soon going to pick up. This can also be a warning against getting into difficult situations.

Cards   Beware of tricksters or your own carelessness in financial matters if you see cards in your dream. The suits each have their own meaning: Clubs = deceit; Spades = danger; Diamonds = gain; Hearts = happiness.

Carpenter   This is one of the happiest omens. You will have love, admiration, plenty of spare time, as well as the ability to benefit from all these things.

Carving   If you see yourself carving meat for other people, someone else will reap the rewards from your hard work. If, on the other hand, you are being served, then you will gain from your efforts.

Castle   To dream of a castle indicates a secure future with exciting travel. If you see a ruined castle, be careful of your amorous passions or your anger.

Cat   This shows that there are people around you who wish to betray you and who are not to be trusted. However, if you kill the cat, you will be triumphant over your adversaries. Expect a sudden piece of luck if you chase the cat away.

Cathedral   To see a cathedral from the outside foretells that you will achieve your greatest ambition. Unfortunately, to see the inside of a cathedral means failure but also denotes that you will receive some recompense along the way.

Cattle   Prosperity will come easily to you if you see cattle grazing peacefully. If you are on a cattle drive, you will be successful only through your own industrious efforts. Look after your business interests if the cattle are black or large-horned.

Cave   This is an obstacle dream. If you see yourself in a cave that you are unable to get out of, prepare yourself for an extended period of increased problems and worry. If you manage to find your way out, you can look forward to triumphing over your difficulties. Cave dwellers predict a happy marriage.

Cellar A dry, tidy, and full cellar signifies gains in business matters. If the cellar is damp and smelly or empty, you may be in for some financial problems unless you avert them or change your plans.

Cemetery This is not a bad dream, as it symbolizes that happiness and prosperity will soon come your way. If the cemetery is scruffy and badly maintained, you will still receive the happiness and prosperity, but only after a little difficulty.

Certificate You will achieve your ambitions only by making an effort. You should be more cooperative with colleagues in smaller matters because by doing this you will reap the rewards in the more important ones.

Chains Dreaming of chains tells you that you will soon be unchained from your current worries.

Chair If you see yourself sitting in a comfortable chair, you can expect your life to be comfortable. If the chair is empty, you will receive unexpected news. A rocking chair means that you will receive an unpredicted gain through the efforts of someone else.

Chandelier If the chandelier is lit and sparkling, this foretells of success, but if is unlit, the success will take longer to come. If you or others are putting a chandelier in place or hanging from one, you should not involve yourself in illicit affairs of a sexual nature.

Cheese If you see yourself eating cheese, celebrate—for it means that you will be successful in love. If the cheese is a mild one, it shows that you need a change. If the cheese is one of the strong types, it is a warning that financial or social humiliation is predicted. Grated or dry cheese means luck in your finances. If you see yourself making cheese, anything that you are currently involved in will succeed beyond your wildest dreams.

Cherries Beautiful, succulent, ripe cherries from a tree or seen in a bowl signify that you will be successful in love. If the cherries are green or damaged in any way, do not trust a current romance, as it will all end in tears and frustration.

Chestnuts Eating chestnuts means that you will be happy in all love, friendship, business associations, or dealings with the opposite sex. If you are cooking

the little book of dream symbols

the chestnuts, someone you trust is attempting to exploit you. If you are splitting open the chestnuts, the solution to a current problem will become clear.

Children   To see children of any walking age is a strong indication that happiness is coming.

Chimney   This dream depends on how you see the chimney. If it is a very tall chimney, it is an indication that you will succeed in an unusual kind of achievement. A normal-sized chimney means that good times are ahead.

Good news is on its way to you if you see smoke rising from the chimney.

A chimney that is in disrepair is confirmation that expected problems will occur. If the chimney actually collapses in your dream, you will soon have cause for celebration.

China   China in a good condition is a sign that you can expect wealth and an idyllic situation at home.

Choir   Pleasant news is on the horizon if you dream of a choir in any situation other than a church. A church choir is a warning of small annoyances.

Circus   This denotes exceptional luck in money matters, particularly if children also enter this dream, but you should be wary of how you go about impressing others.

Clams   To dream of eating clams or oysters is an indication that you will have luck in love, but if financial affairs are at the forefront at the time of having this dream, you will have to assert yourself more if you want to attain success. If you are opening the clams or oysters, a friend will cheat you.

Cleaning   This is a clear warning dream. The harder and faster you appear to be cleaning, the more vital the warning against becoming involved in anything that is unethical, even if it appears to be enjoyable or advantageous.

Clock   This is a simple warning for you to stop wasting time. If you hear the clock chime in your dream, you can improve your situation by being more positive. If you are winding a clock, you can look forward to a happy love affair.

the little book of dream symbols

Closet To see a full closet indicates unusually large benefits in business profits. An empty closet warns of getting yourself into debt. A full linen closet indicates that your family life will be very happy. An empty one suggests that family quarrels are not too far ahead.

Cloth Cotton suggests that you should be careful about losing your reputation through your own behavior. Linen foretells of an increase in your finances. Wool brings a promise of security. Velvet or brocade indicates success in love matters. Silk shows that you will have a pleasant social life.

Clouds A few white clouds within a blue sky tell that better times are ahead. A bank of white clouds within a blue sky foretells that you will have great fun with a member of the opposite sex. Sunnier financial events are ahead if you see the sun go behind the clouds. Stormy clouds in a dark sky indicate sadness to come through a friendship that will be broken.

Clown Expect to be irritated, because your actions will be misinterpreted.

Coat The meaning to dreaming of a coat depends upon the condition that the coat is in during your dream. A new coat indicates a reversal in business matters. An old coat in poor condition suggests wealth or luck in matters concerning money. Losing a coat means you have a false friend. Lending or giving a coat away means you will increase your circle of friends. Hanging up a coat predicts success in business power struggles. Helping someone on with a coat shows that you will be asked for a loan. If someone helped you on with your coat, you will borrow money.

Cobweb Luck is coming to you if you see the cobwebs where you might expect them to be, such as in an attic or a cellar. However, if they are seen elsewhere, you can expect problems due to aggressive competition—unless you are able to get rid of the cobwebs.

Coffee If the coffee is pleasant to drink, good news is on the way, but if it is bitter, you need to break up a friendship. If you are grinding coffee beans, rare domestic happiness is in the cards. If you see coffee being spilled, you will experience a succession of minor disappointments.

Coffin If the coffin contains a body, this predicts sadness but not grief. If the body you see in the coffin is your own, good luck is on its way to you. An empty coffin means that you will probably lose a friend.

Colors Each color has its own meaning:

Mixed You will have increased security and success.

Blue You will be free of worry, and you can expect help from others.

Red You should control your temper.

Green Expect news from afar or plan for a journey.

Gray You will experience a stagnant period.

Mauve You will have some small disappointments.

Orange Delays will occur.

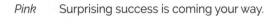

Pink	Surprising success is coming your way.
Yellow	Achievement will be gained only after a series of setbacks and struggle.
White	This color promises success in all areas of your life.
Black	This color is an unhappy omen, unless connected with a funeral, in which case it predicts that you will have difficulties to overcome.

Comb   You will need to push yourself into taking positive action if you see yourself combing your own hair. Combing someone else's hair warns you to be wary of whom you trust. Seeing someone else using a comb foretells that you should stand firm when disassociating yourself from someone in whom you have lost interest. Losing a comb shows that you are becoming disillusioned with a love interest. Lending or borrowing a comb predicts that you will acquire the assistance of someone else in order to sort out financial problems.

Confusion If your dream has an air of confusion about it, it is a warning to you that you should remain on your present path because any changes you may be thinking about will not be beneficial. If the dream is about your own confusion, it foretells that something you had hoped for long ago will come to you again.

Contract To see yourself signing a contract foretells that a promotion is imminent for you. If you refuse to sign the contract, the promotion will be far greater than you expected.

Convict Whether you are the convict in your dream or not, this predicts that you will soon be free of the difficulties currently around you—unless an escape is contained within the dream, in which case minor irritations can be anticipated from someone you least expect. To see yourself convicted denotes that financial gain will soon be coming your way.

Cooking This is one of the luckiest dreams to have. Anything to do with cooking promises material comfort for you in the not too distant future.

Corn This is a lucky dream as it indicates that you will achieve success and happiness in all that you do.

Corpse If the corpse you see is not your own, this foretells of a long and happy life. If the corpse is of someone you know, expect separation or unhappiness in a love affair. If several corpses are seen, success will be yours when you least expect it.

Cough This is a warning dream of fire, flood, theft, or carelessness. Make sure your insurance is up to date.

Court To see a courtroom in your dream foretells of forthcoming financial problems. If you are able to avoid wasting your energy and time on fruitless projects, then the outlook is quite positive.

Cow To see a cow that is happily chewing a cud, grazing in a field, or being milked predicts good luck in all things. If the cow is in poor condition or is angry, or if it chases you, there is a danger that your plans will go awry. If you escape the attack on you, you will overcome any problems. If you are injured or trapped by the cow, prepare yourself for a time of hard work with little reward.

Crab   This is a warning dream. Beware of tricksters in both business and love affairs. If you eat the crab, it indicates that this is a good time for you to take your chances with a small gamble.

Crash   This is a contrary dream. Whatever the cause of the crash in your dream, this is an indication of an important achievement. The more severe the crash, the more significant the achievement.

Cripple   To see yourself as a cripple indicates that you will receive help from others as and when you need it. To see others crippled means the opposite.

Crocodile   You will be the victim of some manipulation by your business colleagues. If the crocodile comes after you, good luck will soon come to you. If the crocodile injures you, expect business losses and disappointment. If you kill one or see a dead crocodile, you can expect accomplishments beyond your wildest dreams.

Crossroads To see a crossroads in your dream means exactly what it appears to mean—you have reached a crossroads and need to make a vital decision. Follow your own intuition and come to the final decision yourself.

Crying If you hear a baby crying, this is a lucky omen, but crying adults show that a friend will soon need your help.

Cup A full cup suggests an improvement in finances, but an empty cup is the reverse. If the cup is patterned or decorated, it is a warning that you should listen to a trusted friend, as you are about to humiliate yourself.

Custard Oh, dear! To dream of custard predicts that you are in for a long period of boredom and dissatisfaction. Hang in there.

Cut Whether you see yourself or others cut themselves, it is a warning to be discreet and to watch how you behave.

Cyclone   This is a warning dream. For the next six months, do not take any unnecessary chances.

Cymbals   Hearing this instrument in your dream is a strong indication that you will soon have a new passionate romance in your life.

Dagger   If you see a dagger in your dream, you can expect to hear some news from afar. If you see yourself carrying a dagger, you should be extremely prudent in all your actions or you will become embroiled in a distasteful situation. To see others with a dagger or someone stabbing another person with a dagger indicates that you will be victorious over any opposition.

Dam   If you see water cascading over a dam, it is a warning that you should guard against impetuous action, especially in relation to any investments or changing your job. You would do well to modify your plans.

Dance   If you see yourself dancing in your dream, everything you are currently involved in will thrive. To see young people dancing together means that you should be happy, as it is an indication that you will be very successful in affairs of the heart. If you see children dancing, look forward to receiving unexpected happiness.

Danger   If you face the danger in your dream, this is an indication that you will overcome any problems you may be experiencing. If the danger is against you in a physical way and you are able to save yourself, take it as a warning that you should guard your health.

Deafness   Do not worry if you dream that you are the one who is deaf, as this predicts financial success. If others are deaf, a solution to any difficulties you may be experiencing is at hand. If you see yourself attempting to communicate with someone who is deaf, you are in for a time of irritation before you can achieve your ambitions.

Death   This is a contrary dream. If you are the one who is dead, you can expect to be freed from all your problems or to have an upturn in your health. To dream of death generally and frequently portends that you will soon hear of a birth. If you speak to someone who is dead, good news will soon be coming, maybe in the form of an inheritance.

Deed   If you dream of a signed deed or see yourself signing one, this is a warning that you should not take any chances with either your personal relationships

the little book of dream symbols

or your finances. If the deed is unsigned or you refuse to sign it, take it as a warning to keep your private matters to yourself.

Deer   To see a deer in its natural habitat indicates that a new friendship will become a solid and pleasant one. If the deer is elsewhere, or in captivity, prepare to be disappointed and upset by a friend letting you down. If you kill a deer or see one dead, it is a warning to beware of a twofaced friend.

Delay   Unfortunately, time delays in a dream indicate that you are about to encounter family upsets. If transport is delayed, problems are about to surface in connection with your finances. I can corroborate this one, as a friend dreamed constantly of airport delays and such; then she left her husband for someone else and lost most of her money as a result. However, she is happy with her new man, and they are now getting on their feet again.

Desert   To see a desert in its natural state and in sunshine indicates satisfaction and success in all that you do. If the weather is bad, and particularly if there is a sandstorm, you will encounter immediate problems due to concealed hostility. However, you will be pleasantly surprised at the outcome.

Desertion To dream of deserting someone or something predicts that you will lose a friend because of thoughtless gossip. If you are the one who is deserted, you have friends who are reliable when you need their help.

Desk If you see an open desk in your dream, contentment is yours in all areas of your life. If the desk is closed, this indicates that you will be upset by a friend or romantic partner. To see yourself going through a desk or cleaning it predicts that you will be meeting new and powerful friends.

Destroy If you see yourself breaking anything within your dream, this is not a good sign, and you will have a hard time for a while, particularly if the goods that you break belong to someone else. If you only discover something broken or destroyed, you will receive an unexpected success. To see the destruction of structures, buildings, or the environment through violence is a strong warning that you should keep a check on your temper, as any form of impulsiveness on your part now will cost you very dearly.

Devil If you meet the devil in your dream and it is a pleasant meeting, a medical checkup is advised. If, however, you see yourself fighting him off, this indicates that you will triumph over those who are attempting to do you harm. If you speak to the devil, you will find it hard to resist temptation.

Dice For a woman to have this dream, it is a stern warning that she should not enter into the romantic relationship that she is contemplating. For a man, it is a severe warning that he should not rush into the financial situation he is going after, as it would be too costly, and that he should approach things at a slower pace. To see others throwing winning dice means that a small financial gain can be expected.

Diploma For a man to dream of a diploma foretells of excellence through his own endeavors. For a woman, it is a warning not to be too vain or wasteful, as it will only end in tears.

Dirt If you dream of having dirt thrown at you or if you are throwing it yourself, it is a warning that a trusted friend is about to betray you. If you or your clothes are dirty, a medical checkup is advised. If you step or fall into dirt, this indicates that you will change your place of residence and that the new place will be an improvement for you.

Discovery To discover someone or something in your dream is a strong indication that you will soon hear of an inheritance coming to you. If you are the one who is discovered, get ready to pack your suitcases, as travel and meeting new people are on the horizon.

Disease This is a contrary dream. To see disease in your dream indicates that you can look forward to some joyous times ahead. If you see someone you know with a disease, you can let them know that good luck is about to be theirs.

Disfigure If you see yourself with a disfiguration, you are in for an unexpected happy time. If you see others disfigured, it is a warning that you are about to be deceived or tricked by someone you normally trust, and that you should avoid getting involved with friends in connection with business.

Dislocation   If you dream that you have a dislocated joint, it is a warning that you should think extremely carefully and look thoroughly at any offer that would involve your changing your employment or place of residence.

Diving   Dreaming of diving is a warning of a future temptation or test. If the water is clear, you will be pleased with the result. However, if the water is dark or rough, you will suffer nasty consequences.

Divorce   If you are married and have this dream, it confirms that your partner can be trusted. If you are single, it is a warning that you have misplaced your affections.

Dock   To dream of a busy dock or dockyard fore-tells of an increase in your finances. If you are stand-ing alone on the dock, or you are seen by someone, you will experience a period of unhappiness. If you are standing on board a ship looking at the dock, you can expect a surprising upturn in your situation.

Doctor A wonderful dream to have—and it does not mean that you need to visit one. It is a strong indication that improvement is about to come to you in all areas of your life.

Dog This is an indication that you have loyal friends and that you are in for some luck. If the dog is friendly and loving, you will have happy times with friends. If it appears fierce and if it is baring its teeth, there will be arguments with friends. It the dog attacks you and bites you, it is a warning to keep alert for betrayal among your friends. To see dogs fighting means that you will intervene between feuding friends, but be careful you are not the one whom they turn against. If the dog is extraordinarily large, a friend in a powerful position will protect you. To hear a dog barking normally indicates appreciation on a social level. If the dog is barking fiercely, it is a warning of possible forthcoming legal problems.

Dolphin To see dolphins in your dream is a message that you need to use a bit of intelligence.

Dominoes If you see yourself playing this game, do not take any risks over the next few months. If you see the dominoes in their box, it is a warning that you should avoid buying anything for the time being.

Donkey   Riding or sitting on a donkey is a good indication that you will be happy in affairs of the heart. If the donkey is stubborn, then you can expect the same reaction from your partner. To hear a donkey bray is a warning that your affair will come out into the open and will cause you embarrassment.

Door   To see an open door, particularly if it opens out onto a panoramic view, foretells of the success of your greatest wishes. A closed or locked door signifies that you will experience regret over missed opportunities. Many doors symbolize a choice among several good prospects.

Drawers   To dream of a drawer that is open means that you should prepare yourself for something new. If the drawer is closed, you will have to use all your ingenuity to obtain what you want. A full drawer indicates that the time is right to start a new venture. An empty drawer foretells that you will achieve what you want but only through your own efforts. A locked drawer is a warning that unseen problems are in your way, but through persistence and patience, you can overcome them.

Drink   To see yourself drinking clear water or any cold drink is very lucky, especially if you happen to be a student, as it foretells that you will gain your academic achievements. If the drink is hot or unpalatable, it is a warning to expect losses due to unfortunate circumstances. If the drink is milk, you will achieve success. Fizzy drinks indicate that you have some excitement coming to you. Sweet drinks are an indication that a passionate affair is about to be yours. If you are drinking from a bottle, expect to have a disappointing experience in love.

Drive   If you are the one doing the driving, it is a warning to be extremely cautious with your financial affairs over the next few weeks, and that you should not gamble. If someone else is doing the driving, you will have some luck concerning money.

Drown   This is not a lucky dream, as it relates to your business interests. The meaning is less worrying if someone rescues you, as you will be able to recoup something.

Drugs If you are the one who is drugged to the extent that it affected your behavior, it is a severe warning that there is someone around you who is very jealous of you and will attempt to manipulate you in order to receive monetary gain. Be extremely cautious in all your actions following a dream of this kind.

Drums To play the drums in your dream predicts great happiness. To hear drums being played predicts success. Seeing drumsticks without the drum, or seeing them being used on anything but a drum, is a warning that you should be extremely honest in all your dealings, in both what you say and what you do; otherwise it could backfire on you. To eat a drumstick from a bird indicates good luck.

Drunkenness To see yourself as drunk is a warning to you that you should slow down and not indulge in too much high living. To see others drunk foretells that a loan will not be repaid to you.

Ducks It is lucky to dream of ducks—unless they attack you, in which case you can expect a small loss that will not necessarily be a financial one. If you see ducks flying, you can expect to receive a financial gain. If they are swimming, you will have a happy family. If you see a duck and drake together, you can expect to receive some happy news of a romantic nature.

Dynamite If you see or hear dynamite exploding, it is a warning that you should give up on a new plan or venture. To be aware of unexploded dynamite in your dream is an indication that anything you have been worrying about will be fine.

Earrings For a woman, this means that you should not repeat gossip. For a man, wearing earrings denotes that interesting developments at work are about to occur.

Earthquake This is a rare dream. If you experience an earthquake, you will have unexpected problems to overcome, but if you see others being shaken, a complete change of environment is in the cards.

Eating Eating with others signifies good luck and abundance in all things, but if you eat alone, you are in danger of losing friends.

Education If you are being educated, you will achieve commercial success, but if you lack an education, you will obtain recognition of a cultural nature.

Eggs Generally, domestic bliss or financial security is indicated. Eating eggs means that you will have good health. Finding eggs indicates that an unexpected monetary gain is about to be yours. Broken or damaged eggs mean that you will experience disappointment through misplaced trust.

Elephant   Elephants bring good luck. You will have to put on a performance or presentation, and helpful friends and colleagues will be around to help. Otherwise, dreaming of elephants signifies improvements or the return of something you thought you had lost. If the elephant frightens or attacks you, expect to experience temporary setbacks.

Elevator   Moving up is good, while moving down is bad.

Embarrassment   This contrary dream shows that the greater the embarrassment, the greater your success will be. If others are embarrassed, rely on your own intuition and do not be swayed by others.

Embrace   When others embrace you, it is a warning to be careful of your behavior. If you see others being embraced, you will have a united family, despite petty arguments.

Embroidery   Doing this yourself indicates happiness and contentment, but if others are embroidering, there is deception around you.

Envelope   Whether the envelope is open or closed, small problems can be overcome so long as you maintain your sense of humor.

Eraser   Do not repeat gossip or it will backfire on you. This can also suggest that you will soon remove yourself from a particularly difficult situation. A friend of mine dreamed that an eraser was rubbing her out and that her family circle would soon not include her. A few weeks later, she walked out on her rotten marriage and left the rest of the family to reorganize itself.

Escape   If you escape from danger, you will have romantic or social success, and if you escape from prison, you can expect to see rapid progression. If the escape is from fire or water, this indicates success but only after a time of anxiety. If you are unable to escape, there will be challenges ahead. If you attempt to escape but someone catches you, the dream advises you to guard your tongue.

Execution   To dream of an execution means unsatisfactory news concerning a friend or colleague, and you will soon need to spend more than you

the little book of dream symbols

anticipated. To be condemned means pleasant news concerning your health.

Exhibition   Attending or working at an exhibition signifies that minor obstacles are in your way, but they will soon move out of the way, so you must be patient.

Explore   If you dream of exploring new territory, you must take time to study details carefully.

Eyebrows   Arched eyebrows indicate that a surprise is coming. Thin eyebrows denote disappointment in love or business matters. Heavy eyebrows forecast excellence and success. If your own eyebrows are falling out or if you are worrying about them in your dream, you are being deceived in love. If you are pleased with their appearance, a minor gain is coming.

Eyes   Beautiful eyes signify that you can rely on your loved ones. Large eyes mean that you can expect an inheritance. Blue or light eyes denote that a new friend is coming. Dark eyes show that a new love affair is on the horizon. Strange eyes bring a beneficial change your way, while crossed eyes mean that luck is coming in money. If you see a squint, there is a warning that you should avoid jumping into a love affair. Injured eyes suggest that you will experience deception in business matters. Animals' eyes symbolize jealousy among your friends.

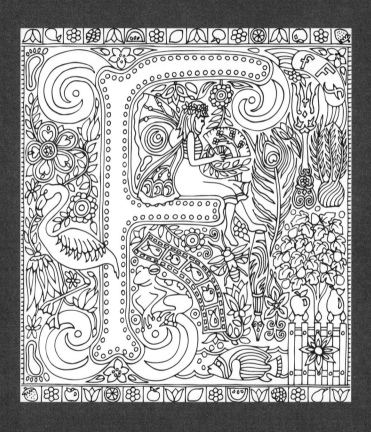

Face If the face that you see is smiling, you will experience pleasure in all areas of your life, but if it is unpleasant or ugly, you will have losses. Seeing the face of others or of strangers forecasts a change of address, while if you are washing your face, you will have to be accountable for past indiscretions.

Factory Dreaming of working in a factory forecasts a beneficial change in your life. If you are very busy, you will achieve a great deal but only after a difficult struggle.

Fairy This is a lucky symbol, and it may mean that your guardian angel or even that "the little people" are looking after you, so there should soon be an unexpected realization of your dreams.

Fall Most people dream of falling at some point in their lives, often falling down stairs. There is a psychological reason for this, which is linked to a lack of self-confidence or temporary feelings of insecurity. You fear that you will not be able to stay on your feet in a particular situation or that you will fall on your face. In more traditional dream interpretations, the meaning is similar to the psychological one, as this indicates a fear of failure. If your fall is a long-distance one, such as falling from an aircraft or off a cliff, you are right to be worried, because your problems will be severe. Landing without ill effects means that the setbacks will only be temporary ones, but if you are hurt, you will suffer severe hardships. If you see others falling, you will outsmart enemies. If you get up after a fall, you will overcome obstacles, but if you fall into water, communication or financial difficulties are ahead.

Fame   Achieving fame signifies that you need to be realistic about your long-term aims. Dreaming about a famous person suggests that you will get help from where you least expect it.

Family   Things will now start to move in an upward direction for you.

Fang   Severe family problems are about to befall you, and you would do well to avoid contact with relatives for the time being if possible.

Farm   If the farm is well kept and flourishing, you can look forward to abundance in all areas. If the farm is neglected and unkempt, this warns of loss.

Fashion   Looking at fashionable clothes shows that you will be working hard and unable to enjoy social pleasures.

Fear   If you overcame the fear, you will also overcome any difficulties that you have, but if the fear persists, you will have to deal with problems created by someone you trusted who is dishonest. Calming others' fears means that misunderstandings will be cleared away.

Feast   The interpretation for this dream depends upon your age. If you are young or middle-aged, good things will come to you, but if you are elderly, you will have some unexpected financial problems.

Feet   Cold feet predict disappointment in love, and dirty feet say that you must guard your finances. Large feet indicate good health, and small feet suggest that you are worrying needlessly. Sore feet show that you will be comfortable in old age. If others step on your feet, they are being indiscreet. Washing your feet signifies that your anxieties will soon disappear.

Fence   There will be obstacles and difficulties ahead.

Field   Large, open, and green fields depict abundance that is coming in all areas of your life. Dry and barren fields show that reversals are heading your way. Newly plowed fields mean that a sacrifice will have to be made for you to gain what you want.

Fight   This dream signifies changes in relation to who you are and what you do. Seeing others fighting means that you must stop wasting your time and money on incidentals.

Fingernails   If the fingernails are long, there are problems ahead with the opposite sex. If the fingernails are short, you will receive a surprising gift. If they are polished, this is a warning that you should be careful about the things that you become involved in, as they could end in scandal. If the fingernails are damaged, a long period of dissatisfaction is about to strike.

Fingers   If the fingers are pointing, you will not stay where you are currently living. If they are cut or damaged, prepare yourself for a period of hard work. If they are very long, you will have an upset in your romantic life, and if they are very short, new friends are heading toward you.

Fire   If you are burned, this is an indication that trouble lies ahead. If you are unscathed, good news is on its way. A fire in a house or building denotes that you will be asked for urgent help from a friend or relation. Building or stoking a fire suggests that a thrilling romantic affair is coming. Putting out or escaping from a fire means that you will overcome all your difficulties.

Fireworks   This is an obstacle dream. You will be held back and have to overcome challenges before you can achieve what you want.

Fish   Fish are a good-luck sign that shows you will achieve both financial and personal power.

Fist   If you are fighting off an aggressor, your career or business will improve, but if you are being hurt, you must be on guard against potential danger.

Flags Your own country flag means that you can look forward to enjoyable social events. Raising or carrying a flag predicts that you can look forward to financial improvement.

Flashlight Used outside, a flashlight means that a new and powerful friend will come to your aid. If you are using the flashlight indoors, this warns you not to enter into any kind of illicit behavior, even though you may be tempted by what seems like a good idea at the time.

Fleas Fleas foretell that there is deception and spite around you. To kill a flea indicates that you will triumph over your adversaries.

Flies If you dream of flies, there is jealousy and envy around you.

Flood If the water is clear, your difficulties will not last for very long. Muddy or raging water means that you will have to work extremely hard. If a flood sweeps you away, the dream means that a member of the opposite sex in whom you have placed your trust is manipulating you for his or her own purposes.

If you escape from a flood, this means that others will help you to get through your difficulties.

Florist   If you are married or committed, this warns of a serious split. If you are unattached, you can expect to enter into a serious new romance.

Flowers   Fresh flowers are a wonderful sign that happiness will be yours. Dead or dying flowers warn that you must watch your ego, as pride comes before a fall. Artificial flowers suggest that you should follow your own intuition and refuse to be swayed by others. Wildflowers indicate that enthralling times are ahead.

Football   Playing football means that a financial gain is coming your way. Watching football warns that you must be choosier about your friends.

Forest   If you are well off and you dream of becoming lost in a forest, this warns of a loss, but if you are not rich, you can expect to receive some gain. If you dream that you are alone or frightened while in the forest, someone you currently rely upon will let you down. If you dream that you are hiding in a forest, do not worry about any difficulties you may currently be experiencing, as you will eventually benefit from them.

Fork In relation to eating, a fork signifies that your worries will soon disappear. If you dream of a garden fork, it is time for you to rid yourself of hangers-on in your circle of friends. A fork in the road means that you will soon be faced with a major decision. To stab someone with a fork or to see someone stabbed with one is a warning to watch what you say, as it could lead to your downfall.

Fountain If the fountain is functioning, this signifies a happy and contented life, but if it is malfunctioning, prepare yourself for a time of frustration.

Freckles Whatever your age, you will become more attractive to the opposite sex.

Freedom You will be contented with the partner of your choice and you will experience great happiness.

Friends If you dream of true friends, you are in for some delightful social events. If your friends are at a distance, news is coming your way; the kind of news will be dependent upon how you see your friends and whether any trouble is involved.

Frost If you see patterns of frost on trees or on a window, you are in for a surprising and curious experience. If you are frostbitten, you need to exert caution in all areas of your life.

Fry Frying anything foretells of unhappiness in matters of love. If you burn food, someone will raise your spirits.

Funeral Attending your own funeral symbolizes that you will soon be relieved of all of your anxieties, but if the funeral is for someone else you will have reason to celebrate.

Fur Owning or wearing fur indicates that better times are ahead. Damaged fur suggests that your status will change, but this will not affect your finances.

Furniture Purchasing furniture means that you need to be flexible and to adapt to something you do

the little book of dream symbols

not like. Selling furniture indicates small monetary problems. If the furniture in your dream is better than what you already own, you can expect to be comfortable in the future. Dilapidated furniture means that romantic or marital problems are ahead. Opulent furniture warns that you should work within your means and avoid attempting anything that is beyond your ability.

Gag   Getting rid of a gag or speaking through it predicts that difficulties will be overcome. Seeing others gagged means that you should avoid getting yourself embroiled in gossip or you will end up having to defend yourself.

Gallery   To see paintings in a gallery foretells that you will renew a friendship from the past. If you see sculptures, this is not a time to speculate, as you will lose. A gallery of an observatory type predicts that the project you are currently working on will be successful. To fall from a gallery means that you will quarrel with your partner.

Gambling   If you dream of winning, it is a warning not to risk anything you cannot afford to lose. To see yourself losing means that an advantageous opportunity will soon come your way.

Gangway   If the atmosphere is happy when you see a gangway, your future will be much easier than the past has been. A distressful atmosphere denotes that any changes you make could become stressful.

Garage   To see your own garage signifies that you will have security through your own hard work. If the garage is empty, you are about to be deceived by someone you trust. A public garage indicates an increase in your general affairs.

Garbage   You will achieve success beyond your wildest dreams.

Garden   Dreaming of a garden in bloom means that you will be abundant in all areas, including spiritual ones. If the garden is well maintained, a comfortable life can be expected, but you will also experience minor problems along the way. If the garden is unkempt, this indicates hardships to come.

Garland   If you are wearing a garland, you need to get your thinking cap on, as this will help you to triumph over any problems. Receiving a garland indicates that you will make steady progress. Giving one is a warning against untrustworthy associates.

Garlic   You are on the way up and you should be able to achieve prominence and wealth.

the little book of dream symbols

Gas Station If you purchase gasoline, you can expect your finances to improve. Selling gasoline indicates that patience is required because you are facing reversals in business. Using the washroom at a gas station happily shows that your problems are about to disappear. Running out of gas foretells that you will suddenly gain clarity and enthusiasm.

Gate If you see the gate open, new opportunities are coming your way. If the gate is closed, this predicts that you will overcome obstacles as long as you see yourself being able to open the gate. If the gate is locked, insoluble problems are around you—unless you are able to get through the gate in any way, in which case the problems will be temporary.

Gem Dreaming of gems and gemstones is always lucky as it is an omen of wealth and happiness.

Ghetto Dreaming of being in a ghetto is a warning against overspending.

Ghost Dreaming of ghouls and ghosts has various meanings. If the dream is a happy one, your future will be bright, but if you were frightened or warned by the ghost, you must avoid becoming involved in something that will bring trouble your way.

Giant This is great for financial and business matters.

Gift Giving a gift in your dream is an indication that you are about to receive some happy news. Receiving a gift warns that you must be aware of what is being offered to you, as it is not what it seems.

Gin Dreaming of this spirit represents a time of confusion and loss.

Girl To see a girl you recognize indicates good prospects ahead. If the girl is a stranger, you are about to receive some unexpected news.

Glacier If you see or walk across a glacier, you will be receiving some important news that will be coming from a distance, or you could actually be going on a long journey. Falling into a crevasse is a stern warning that you are about to enter into something that might become extremely dangerous.

Glass   If the glassware seen in your dream is clean, you can look forward to some good luck, but if it is dirty, some disagreements are coming. If the glassware is broken, changes are about to take place. Polishing glassware is a warning not to be too overconfident.

Gloves   Wearing gloves in your dream is an indication of emotional security. Losing the gloves means that you need to rely on yourself, as someone will let you down. Finding gloves indicates that you will receive assistance from an unexpected quarter. To see new gloves predicts that you will have financial security. Old and worn gloves indicate temporary setbacks.

Glue   Something will need to be handled very carefully, so caution is advised.

Goat   A goat is a warning for you not to get involved in anything at the moment unless you can see that it is improving. To see yourself chased or frightened by a goat is a stern warning for you not to gamble.

Gold   If you handle gold in your dream, this is an indication that you will be amazingly successful. If you marry soon, your husband will be rich. If you are not in good financial shape right now, you soon will be.

Goldfish   This is an omen of success and a happy relationship.

Golf   Playing or watching a good game of golf is an indication that your love life will go from strength to strength. If the conditions or the game is not good, then you must expect heartache.

Gondola   A romance or a romantic holiday is indicated.

Gong   A gong foretells a period of healing if you have been sick. You can also expect a pleasant event and a change for the better.

Goose   To see this bird in flight denotes that an unexpected trip is forecast. If it is swimming, you will receive an unexpected visitor. Hearing the sound of a goose or geese warns that you must guard against gossip. Plucking a goose suggests that your circumstances are about to take an upturn. Catching this bird indicates that you will receive some sad news, while seeing geese in a flock tells you that someone is being two-faced.

Gossip If the gossip is about you, pleasant news is on its way. If you or others are doing the gossiping, expect domestic arguments to arise. If you are accused of gossiping, it is .a strong warning not to do any gossiping yourself.

Government Whether local or national, this indicates a period of uncertainty.

Graduation Seeing or being in a graduation ceremony shows that you can expect to receive acclaim in social and business ranking.

Grain A dream that involves any type of grain or seeds indicates wealth, security, and happiness. Grains have meant this from the beginning of time, and even Joseph (the one with the coat of many colors) interpreted the dream in this way when the Pharaoh dreamed of grain piling up in his storehouses.

Grandparent   Grandparents are an omen of protection and security.

Grapes   If you dream of eating or picking grapes, you are too engrossed in thoughts of a sexual nature. If you see the grapes growing or being collected, prosperity and comfort will be yours.

Grasshopper   This insect indicates indecision and advice that confuses and conflicts.

Grave   This is not a good dream to have. To see a new grave that has flowers upon it signifies a broken promise. If the grave is neglected, you will have heartache. To see an open grave tells that you will receive unhappy news from afar. To see yourself digging a grave or to see your own grave is a warning that you will be frustrated by a hidden enemy. If you fall into a grave, you are about to lose a friendship.

Gravestone   This is a contrary dream. To see a new gravestone indicates that there is a new opportunity coming your way. To see old gravestones foretells that you will renew an old friendship.

the little book of dream symbols

Grief   This is a contrary dream. If you dream of grieving, you will soon have reason for celebration.

Guard   To see anything being guarded is a warning against loss through either your own carelessness or even theft. If you dream of being on guard, you can look forward to an increase in your finances.

Gum   Seeing or chewing gum in your dream is a stern warning that you should not divulge anything to new friends and you should not enter into casual affairs. If you see yourself undergoing treatment on your gums, you will have a disturbing argument that could lead to a rift. If the gums are not in a healthy condition, expect family and personal problems. Dreams of teeth and gums are surprisingly common.

Gun   To see a gun in any situation foretells that you are in for a difficult time and that you will have to fight to overcome the problem. If you see yourself loading a gun, it is a warning for you to guard your temper.

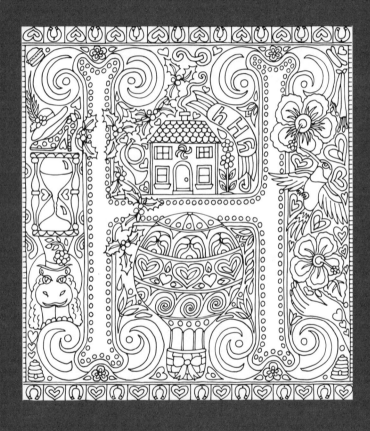

Hair   The meaning of this dream is dependent upon how you see the hair.

◊   If it is thick and healthy, you can expect contentment and progress in your life.

◊   If it is thin or lank, this is a warning that you have difficulties to face.

◊   To see yourself combing or brushing your hair tells that you will solve a current problem.

◊   Combing or brushing someone else's hair denotes that a friend will ask for your help.

◊   Seeing your own hair cut, whether by you or by someone else, means that you will achieve success in your new venture.

◊   To cut someone else's hair is a warning that you have untrustworthy people around you.

◊   Braiding your own hair foretells that you are about to make a new friend.

◊   Braiding someone else's hair foretells that you are about to have an argument with someone.

◊   Curling your hair is an indication that your affairs of the heart are about to improve.

◊   Having your hair done at the hairdresser is a warning that you should not enter into gossip.

◊   To see hair growing on other parts of your body is a strong indication that you will receive a gradual increase in your financial matters.

Hall   To see a normal-sized entrance hall indicates that you will have to overcome minor but irritating problems. If the hall is large and elegant, changes are coming to you. A long, narrow hall is a warning that you are about to experience a long period of anxiousness. A public hall indicates that you now need to make that important decision you have so far been putting off.

Ham   If you are eating ham in your dream, you can expect to have luck in all of your business matters. Baking the ham means that good fortune will ultimately be yours after a short period of difficulty. If you are cooking the ham by smoking, the year ahead will be extremely prosperous for you.

Hammer   If you use a hammer in your dream, you will accomplish what you set out to do. To see or hear a hammer in any situation means that you can expect some good luck.

Hammock   If you see yourself alone in a hammock, it is a warning that you should not be selfish or you will lose friends. If you are in the hammock with someone of the opposite sex, you will be going to more social events. If you fall out of the hammock, it is a warning that you should make more effort and not take your partner for granted.

Hand   The interpretation of seeing a hand or hands in your dream is dependent on its condition.

◊   Clean and well-manicured hands are an indication that you will have a contented life.

◊ Unpleasant or dirty hands are a stern warning that you should be careful as to how you behave or your behavior may backfire on you.

◊ Large hands indicate that you will have sexual satisfaction, whereas small hands predict infidelity.

◊ If you see a right hand, pleasure is on its way to you, whereas the left hand foretells of small difficulties that you will find irritating.

◊ Shaking hands is a sign of renewed friendship, but waving means separations.

◊ Seeing hands being washed means that you should rectify a past misdeed.

◊ To see hairy or swollen hands is a strong indication that you will receive some gain in business matters.

◊ If you see your hands tied, you will experience annoying obstacles and you should change your plans.

the little book of dream symbols

Handcuffs Dreams of restriction are a warning not to enter into any situation that will restrict you or make you unhappy. If you place handcuffs on others, you can look forward to surprising improvements in your life.

Hanging If you had this ominous dream, do not worry, as it foretells that you will have a season of good luck. If you are the hangman, this is a stern warning that you should not criticize others; otherwise it will be you who will ultimately be criticized.

Harbor If you dream of leaving a harbor, you will discover that you have a false friend. Entering the harbor is an indication that the future will be secure for you.

Harvest If it is a good harvest, you can expect success in all areas of your life. However, if it is a bad harvest, beware of friends or associates who are attempting to manipulate you for their own benefit.

Hat To see a new hat is a portent of good luck, but if the hat is old and damaged, expect some irritating business problems. If your hat is too small for you,

you are in for a disappointment. If the hat is too big for you, prepare yourself to be embarrassed. Losing your hat or having it blown off your head predicts financial problems. If you find a hat, your worries will disappear as if by magic.

Hatchet   If you see a hatchet in your dream, you are in for a disruptive time in connection with both business and domestic affairs. If the hatchet is used to split wood, you can look forward to reconciliation. If you are sharpening a hatchet, your finances are on the upturn.

Hawk   If the hawk is sitting around, you can expect life to be dull and boring, but if it takes off or if it is flying, you can expect a bright future.

Hay   If you see the hay in sunshine, unfortunately it is not a sunny prediction; it is a warning that you should take a serious look at your finances, as you are on the verge of serious difficulties. However, if the weather is bad at the time of seeing the hay, this foretells of money coming in unexpectedly. To see haystacks is an indication that you will gain where you thought you had lost. Seeing hay being cut foretells that you are in for an uncertain period.

Head   To see your own head in a dream foretells of luck in something that has been causing you concern. A disembodied head indicates that you will have to use your head in order to overcome a problem. To receive a bang on your head is a suggestion that you need to take a break and relax more. To see two heads signifies that you will suddenly receive acclaim for which you will be grateful.

Heart   Dreaming of a heart is a good omen as far as love is concerned, but it is not a good one for health, and it can even be the first indication of a forthcoming heart attack.

Heather   This is an ancient omen of luck, especially in love and money. If the heather was white, the luck will be even better.

Herbs   To see herbs growing foretells that you can look forward to a life of peace and contentment. If you smell herbs, you can look forward to new and exciting events, including foreign travel.

Hero If you are the hero in your dream, you will be heavily criticized by someone you admire. If the hero is someone else, expect to receive a new offer that will prove to be beneficial to you.

Heaven This is good news for anything here on earth.

Hedge If you are cutting a hedge, there is luck and happiness around the corner. If you jumped over it, you may get something that you don't want. Remember the old saying, "Be careful of what you ask for, as you might get it!"

Hide If you are hiding, the message is to not rush into anything new, but if you are hiding an article, this tells you not to be secretive but to allow a trustworthy person to help you.

Highway If the highway is busy, your difficulties are about to increase. If you cross a highway, things will get worse before they get better, but then the problems will completely disappear.

the little book of dream symbols

Hog   If the hog is clean, you can expect to receive success through your own efforts and ability. If the hog is dirty, you can expect an exciting new business proposition. If it is a wild hog in your dream, beware of malicious gossip from someone close to you.

Hole   To see yourself falling into a hole is a warning that you should consider your relationships, as they contain some people you cannot trust. If you are digging a hole, pack your bags, because you are about to embark on a sudden journey. To see a hole in a garment means a financial improvement. Holes that are made by others indicate that you can look forward to an easier time in the future.

Holidays   As with most holidays, to dream of one foretells that you will have to work hard to achieve what you want but that you will get there.

Holly   Holly is a good dream, as it predicts luck in all areas of your life. However, if it pricks you, it is a warning that you should not become involved in anything sinister.

Honey All through the ages, dreaming of honey has been considered an unusually lucky dream, as it predicts sweetness in all areas of your life.

Honeymoon Unfortunately, this indicates disappointments and unhappiness in love.

Horn A horn in your dream is the bringer of good news. If you are blowing the horn, you will be invited out to social events. If you hear the horn of an automobile, it is a warning that you should not take any risks at this time.

Horse Life will be easier, and you can expect more money and an increase in status.

Hospital If you are the patient or are taken to a hospital, you are attempting to deal with a problem yourself that will overburden you; you need—and should ask for—help to solve it. If you are visiting someone in a hospital, amazing news is on its way to you.

Hotel If you stay alone in the hotel, the dream relates to your business and financial matters. If you are there with someone of the opposite sex, then the dream relates to your love life. A luxurious hotel predicts failure in the outcome of an important matter, but a modest hotel shows that you will achieve your aims.

House House dreams are amazingly common, and they always relate to your state of mind at the time of the dream. For instance, a messy house that is filled with irritating people shows that you have too much to do and too many demands being made on you. If the house is clean, peaceful, and attractive, your life is probably easy at the moment and is likely to stay that way.

Hurry Dreaming of being in a hurry, whether you are able to reach your destination or not, shows that you are under too much pressure at the moment and that you must delegate some of your chores.

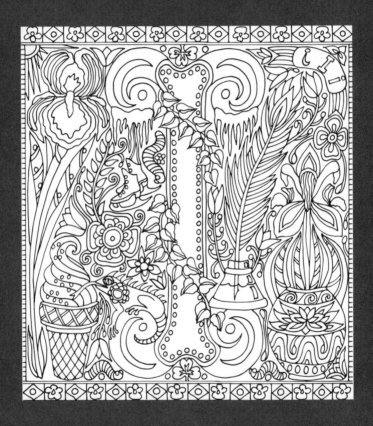

Ice The interpretation of this dream depends on the circumstances:

◊ Walking on ice is a warning that you should not speculate.

◊ To slip, slide, or fall signifies that difficulties are on their way.

◊ If you fall through the ice, this is an indication that you are worrying needlessly.

◊ To sit on the ice foretells that your living conditions will be comfortable.

◊ If you are skating alone on ice, this foretells that you will receive recognition at work.

◊ Seeing yourself skating with someone else is a warning to be discreet about love and sex.

◊ If the ice is the kind that you eat—ice cream—this denotes great success and great advantages to come.

◊ To see icicles foretells that all your problems will soon disappear.

◊   If the icicles are dripping, you are warned to guard your finances for the next few months.

Illness   If you dream that you are ill, unsettling circumstances are predicted for you. To see others ill means that someone will break a promise.

Impatience   If you feel impatient in your dream or if you sense that others are impatient, you will experience confusion within your close circle of friends and family; you should form judgments slowly and carefully.

Infection   If you need advice, you must consult someone who is well qualified.

Inheritance   As the dream suggests, you can look forward to receiving a legacy.

Injury   To dream of a physical injury is a warning that there is a great deal of hostility around you and that you should proceed with extreme caution. If the injury is to your reputation, you can actually look forward to receiving recognition for your efforts.

Insects All insect dreams signify small problems and irritations.

Instruments If the instruments are of a medical kind, this foretells of family quarrels, whereas if they are of any other type, you can look forward to family unity.

Insurance To dream of receiving a payout from an insurance policy indicates setbacks, but if you buy insurance, the plans you have made for the future are sound.

Invitation An invitation received that is written or printed denotes a period of depression or boredom. If you are invited by word of mouth, your social life will be on the upturn.

Iron In astrology, iron is the metal of Mars, so something made of iron suggests that you will soon have some kind of battle on your hands, but you have the ability to win through as long as your courage doesn't desert you. Dreaming of an iron denotes smoothing things over between battling friends or family members.

Island If you see yourself as a castaway on an island, you can expect to feel lonely and isolated. Being rescued or visiting an island means that a new and exhilarating experience will soon come your way.

Itch To dream of yourself or others itching indicates that you are worrying needlessly over problems that do not actually exist. You need to take a more positive approach to life.

Ivy If you see ivy growing on a house, this signifies financial gain coming to you. If it is wrapping itself around a tree, you will be healthy and fit. If the ivy is growing around doors, you have friends you can rely on. If the ivy is growing indoors in pots, happiness is yours.

Jab Dreaming of being jabbed is an indication that you need to believe in yourself more, because your nervousness is hindering your own progression. If you jab at others, the message is to not be too aggressive toward others and to learn a little diplomacy.

Jackal To see a jackal is a warning that you should not allow yourself to be talked into anything by ambitious friends.

Jackpot If you see yourself winning the jackpot, prepare yourself for a period of hard work with little reward at the end of it. To see others winning means that you will gain if you make a little effort.

Jade This is a very ancient symbol of wealth and also of protection, so while you may not become rich, you will certainly be protected from poverty.

Jail If you are released or escape from jail, your difficulties will be short-lived; otherwise expect a long struggle. If you see others in jail, you will soon be free from worry. A friend of mine spent every night for two months prior to her wedding dreaming of being locked away with nobody around to hear her.

the little book of dream symbols

Needless to say, she soon found herself trapped in a difficult marriage.

Jealousy   If you are jealous in your dream, it is a warning of numerous difficulties concerning your marriage or relationship. If someone is jealous of you, any antagonism you are currently experiencing will turn out to your advantage.

Jewelry   If you are wearing jewelry, it is a warning that you should not be so impulsive in your actions. To give or receive, purchase or sell, any jewelry in your dream is an omen for good luck in your domestic and love affairs. To steal the jewelry is a warning that you should pay attention to your business matters. If it is costume jewelry, take heed that your vanity does not lead you into a trap.

Jilting   This is a contrary dream, as if you see yourself being jilted, it foretells that you will have success in your love affairs or consistency within your marriage.

Job   This is a contrary dream. If you see yourself being offered a job, you need to pay more attention to your responsibilities. However, if you lose a job or are looking for a new one, expect a beneficial gain or even a promotion.

Journey   Travel dreams are very common, and they describe your state of mind at the time of the dream. For instance, if the journey is pleasant, you will be happy to take on extra responsibilities. However, if it is fraught with problems, you probably have too much on your plate.

Judge   To see a judge in your dream predicts frustrations, irritations, and problems, but the setbacks will only be of a temporary nature.

Jug   If the jug or jugs are full, this is an indication that you have good friends around you. To drink from a jug foretells of good health and happiness. If the jug is broken, then you can look forward to an exciting new romance or making a new and influential friend.

Juggler   A juggler dream suggests that you are hesitating over an opportunity that can bring you gain or advancement. The message is not to hesitate but to go ahead.

the little book of dream symbols

Juice Drinking juice is an indication that you will receive financial help just when you need it. If you are the one serving the juice, then expect someone to ask you for your help.

Jungle Jüngle dreams are quite common, and the message in them depends upon your experience while in the jungle. For instance, if you enjoy being there, your family relationships and love life will be peaceful and safe. However, if you feel afraid, become entangled in the jungle, or get lost, the dream warns you against starting a romance or an affair right now as it would be a disaster. If you are in a difficult relationship—especially an affair—consider calling it a day and ending it.

Jury Seeing a jury in your dream foretells that you will receive acclaim from those you admire. If you are one of the jurors, it signifies that you should take notice of your own intuition instead of listening to others.

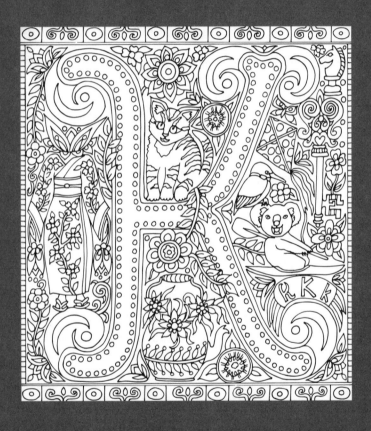

Kangaroo If the kangaroo is jumping along with a baby in its pouch, you can look forward to an unexpected but exciting journey.

Karate If you are learning or doing karate, this shows luck; others doing it warns about obstacles to your plans.

Kennel An influential person who is being pretentious is causing you irritation, but take no notice, as it will be revealed that this person is actually of no consequence to you.

Kettle If the kettle is new, bright, and shiny, you can look forward to domestic bliss, but if it is old or dull, prepare yourself for an unexpected expense.

Keys This is a common dream, and there are various meanings attached to it.

◊ Being given a key predicts help from powerful friends.

◊ If you give someone a key, you can expect improvement in your living conditions.

◊   If you lose a key, you will be very disappointed with a friend, and this could lead to unpleasantness.

◊   If you find a key, you can look forward to solving your problems.

◊   If you see yourself placing a key into a lock, you can smile, because it means that you will be very happy with your love life.

◊   Turning a key in a lock signifies the opening of new doors for you, but to see a broken key means that you will miss out on opportunities.

Kidnap   If you are the one who is kidnapped, it is a warning that you will be embarrassed by your friends and you should reconsider a friendship. If you do the kidnapping, it is a warning to make sure your insurance is up to date, as you are in danger of a loss. If you just observe a kidnapping taking place, this signifies that important changes are about to take place.

Killing   If it is you who is doing the killing, it is a warning that you really must curb your temper, as you are coming into a period of extreme stress. If you witness a killing, it is an indication that changes are coming that you will not like. To see others killing insects or animals means that you can expect to receive help from others, but if you are the one killing these creatures, you will have to be self-reliant in order to overcome your difficulties.

King   If you meet or see royalty in your dream, you can look forward to happiness and a rise in status and prosperity. If the dream has a disagreeable element to it, then take it as a warning that you could become the victim of some malicious gossip.

Kiss   If the kissing in your dream is natural and pleasing, this signifies happiness and satisfaction. If, however, it is of an illicit or obligatory kind, it foretells that you will be let down in a love affair.

Kitchen   To dream of a bright and well-kept kitchen means that you will have all that you need, but if the kitchen is messy and untidy, it is a warning to look after your health.

Kite A flying kite says that you will achieve your highest aims, particularly if children are in the dream. If the string or the kite breaks and the kite flies away, a lack of proper management of your affairs will bring disappointment.

Knapsack To have a full or heavy knapsack in your dream foretells of a pleasant vacation coming. If the knapsack is empty, you will experience financial difficulties for a while.

Knife All dreams of knives and weapons are an indication of danger, loss, an unhappy love life, legal problems, or loss of money.

Knitting If you dream of knitting, you can look forward to a happy and peaceful home life. If you drop any stitches while knitting, expect some family discord.

Labyrinth   If you are in a maze and find your way out, you will overcome problems, but if you are lost or afraid, you will become irritated by something you cannot see; a change of direction is being suggested.

Lace   Hold on to your hat, because to dream of lace means that you will be unusually popular with the opposite sex and will do well in love affairs.

Ladder   Dreaming of going up a ladder indicates good news; going down has the opposite meaning. The height and condition of the ladder shows how far you will go in achieving your ambitions and whether you have obstacles to overcome. Dreaming of going down means that pride comes before a fall.

Lake   A calm lake in sunny conditions foretells a pretty easy life. A turbulent and stormy lake foretells of a failure that, providing you remain calm, will prove to be beneficial to you. Happiness in love will come to you if you dream of a moonlit lake.

Lamp   A lighted lamp in your dream indicates success. To see an unlit lamp suggests disappointments. If you light the lamp, you will receive an unexpected gift for past kindness. If you put a lamp out, then you can look forward to a holiday or period of rest.

Landscape   A beautiful and scenic landscape indicates that your prospects for the future will be good. However, if the landscape is ugly or unpleasant in any way, you must expect a season of discontentment.

Lateness   Dreaming of being late for something is extremely common, and it usually means that you are making too many promises to others. If others are late, it is a warning that you should guard your finances, as you are overextending yourself.

Laughter   To hear laughter in your dream is a strong indication that you will face problems with those in authority. If the laughter is that of children, you can expect to receive some luck in money matters. If you are laughing, this signifies disillusionment in love. If the laughter is that of others, a friendship will be broken.

Laundry   Doing your own laundry signifies you will receive unexpected assistance from someone on whom you made an impression. If you see yourself in a laundromat, a celebration is coming.

Law or Lawyers If you saw yourself involved with the law, you will have some unpleasant experiences in connection with business matters. If you hired a lawyer, it is a stern warning that you should look after your financial affairs more carefully. If you won a case, it is a warning that you are on the losing side of a current argument. If you were sued, do not have that casual love affair you were contemplating. If you dreamt of being a lawyer, you can look forward to receiving some unexpected news.

Leaf To dream of luscious green leaves foretells of abundance. Dry or dead leaves are a warning that you will have to contend with maliciousness. Falling leaves suggest that you will part from friends. Leaves blown by the wind warn of family arguments ahead.

Letter If you receive good news, then the prediction is that you can look forward to good things coming, while the opposite applies if the news is bad. Routine or unimportant letters signify financial problems due to a poor budget.

Library If you are involved in any creative form of activity, then to dream of a library is a lucky omen.

Light   Dreaming of daylight brings renewed hope. Seeing a beam of light signifies that you will suddenly find a solution to an old problem.

Lighthouse   If you see the lighthouse in daylight, then you can look forward to a journey abroad. If you see it at night, good luck in love and business matters is assured.

Lightning   Lightning means a period of exceptionally good luck. However, if accompanied by thunder, there will be a short period of worry before the good luck comes along.

Lion   A lion in your dream foretells that you have the leadership qualities you need to succeed. If you hear a lion roar, you will have to deal with a jealous associate.

Lips   The meaning of this dream is dependent on the shape of the lips. Beautiful lips suggest a satisfying and pleasing sex life. Thin lips warn that you should not be too quick to judge others. Thick lips indicate success in business but not in love.

Lock This predicts that you may need to enlist legal services to sort out family or personal problems. If you pick a lock, it is a warning that you will experience embarrassment due to interfering with someone else's affairs.

Locomotive If you are driving the locomotive, you can expect to succeed in all things. If you are riding in one, it is a sign that you will gain in status or financial matters. If you observe one, you can either expect visitors from abroad or a journey.

Loss To sense that you lost anything in a dream foretells that you should not be too clever for your own good, as you could end up suffering the consequences.

Love To dream of love that is of a natural kind is a good indication that you will have happiness and contentment in that area. If the love is of an illicit type, you will sustain losses through being too greedy. If you observe others making love, it foretells that you will succeed in all that you do.

Machinery If the machinery is in good condition and running smoothly, you can expect achievements. If the machinery malfunctions or is idle, it foretells of forthcoming work or family difficulties.

Market   To be shopping in a busy market indicates that wealth will be yours. However, if the market is empty, you are in for a difficult time ahead, owing to the fact you have ignored opportunities.

Marriage If you are single and have a dream of being married, unfortunately this foretells that you are wasting your time with your current lover and would do well to look elsewhere.

Massage   Having a massage tells you that the suspicions you are having over a friend are unjustified. To dream of giving a massage is an indication that good news is on its way.

Meat   Dreaming of meat is a lucky dream and a good indication that increases in material wealth are on their way to you.

Medal   If you are wearing a medal, you can expect to receive recognition for your work. Placing a medal upon someone else is a warning that you should watch your ego.

Medicine   To take medicine in your dream is a good indication that your troubles are not as bad as you think they are. If you hand out medicine, you will have a tough time before you are able to relax again.

Milk   This is dependent upon the type of milk. Cow's milk indicates good health. Goat's milk indicates success in business matters. Mother's milk is extremely lucky and assures everlasting happiness so long as you are able to apply yourself correctly. Spilled milk is a warning that you are attempting too much. Sour milk warns of self-created problems.

Millionaire   Dreaming that you are a millionaire predicts that a past good deed you did will bring you a repayment. If you meet a millionaire, you are advised to listen to the advice of those who are older and wiser than you.

Mirror   Seeing a reflection of yourself or others in a mirror is a warning for you not to trust your friends.

Money   Paying, giving, or lending money means that you can look forward to things going well. Receiving money is an indication that you will do well through your own efforts.

Moon   This indicates a change for the better in a month's time.

Moth   If you attempt to catch a moth in your dream, you are being warned of hidden jealousy around you. If you catch the moth and destroy it, you will triumph over your enemies. Moth holes in clothing signify disappointments and sadness.

Motor, Engine, Automobile, Motorcycle   Smooth-running motors foretell good progress to come. However, if the motor is troublesome, it suggests that you are not on the right track and that you should reassess your aims. If there is someone else in the dream, this shows the condition of your personal relationships.

Mountain You can expect an increase in either your finances or your status if you dream of climbing a mountain, even if you have to overcome what seem like insurmountable challenges.

Mouse, Mice Conflicts between friends or family are possible.

Mouth To dream of an open mouth is a warning that you should not gossip and that you should be prepared to have an open ear instead. If teeth are showing, it is a warning against a friend who is untrustworthy. A pretty but small mouth foretells money coming your way. A large mouth is an indication that you will make a precious new friend.

Moving If you dream of moving and the move goes well, you will overcome any difficulties you may currently have. If you have problems with the move, then now is the time for you to decide whether or not to economize or make a new start.

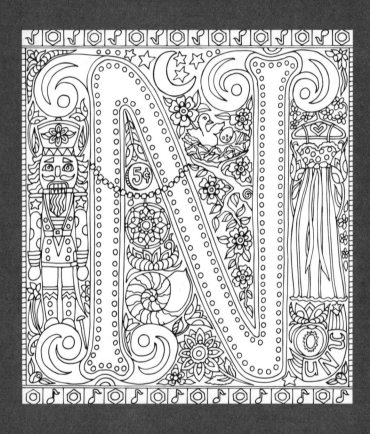

Nagging   If you are being nagged in your dream, it is a warning that you should be extremely careful in whom you confide. If it is you who is doing the nagging, it suggests that you should talk over what is bothering you with a trusted friend.

Nails   To see yourself hammering nails predicts that you will have to work extraordinarily hard to achieve something you first thought you were not able to do. If the nails are new ones, you will receive some unexpected news. However, if they are damaged or rusty, you will experience small setbacks.

Nakedness   Dreams of being naked, insufficiently dressed, or partially dressed in an inappropriate situation are very common. The root of these dreams is insecurity and a lack of self-confidence, probably in the context of something that you are trying to do in your waking life. For instance, you may feel that your job is getting on top of you or that you are unable to cope with people or situations of some other kind. Tradition says that naked dreams are good omens for finances, although if you see others naked, this is a strong indication that you will discover that someone is deceiving you.

Navel To see your own navel in a dream means that you will soon be thinking over a new undertaking that will be beneficial for you. If it is someone else's navel, you can look forward to a forthcoming new love affair.

Necklace Dreaming of a necklace relates to luck in love affairs. A broken necklace, however, indicates romantic upsets and disappointment.

Needles This dream has several interpretations, according to the context.

◊ If you prick yourself with a needle, you will encounter problems from either a relative or a friend who has experienced some bad luck.

◊ If you find a needle, this signifies unnecessary problems.

◊ If you lose a needle, it is a warning that you have jeopardized yourself by your own behavior.

◊ If you thread a needle easily, you will have luck in all of your current projects.

◊ If the needle is difficult to thread, you are in for a time of frustration.

Neighbor If you dream of helping your neighbor, you can look forward to a surprising gift or small financial gain. However, if you fall out with your neighbor, it is a warning that you should watch your temper because it might land you in trouble.

Nervous To have the sensation of feeling nervous in your dream is a warning that you should not be so generous, and that you should look after your finances.

Newspaper If you are purchasing a newspaper, you will rise quickly in your position. If you are reading one, your long-term prospects are good.

Nipple As expected, to dream of nipples is a favorable sexual dream. If a baby is feeding from a nipple, you will soon be free from any worries.

Noise If you hear loud or odd noises in your dream, this is an indication of domestic discord. If the noise actually wakes you from your dream, you can look forward to a change for the better coming.

Nose The interpretation is dependent on how you see or feel the nose.

◊ If you see your own nose, your circle of friends is larger than you think.

◊ Blowing your nose is an indication that you will have a pleasant increase in your responsibilities.

◊ If the nose is swollen, you can look forward to increased material wealth.

◊ If you see a nosebleed, it is a warning that you will experience financial problems and that you must be cautious about lending money over the following months.

Novel If you dream of writing a novel, you can expect problems ahead. If you are reading one, you will receive pleasant social invitations.

the little book of dream symbols

Numbers Seeing or being aware of numbers in a dream is unusual, but if you do see them, it shows that your reputation will improve and you will have more power. If you remember the numbers you dream of, this foretells good luck ahead. If you cannot remember them, you are in for a time of bewilderment and uncertainty concerning other people.

Nurse To see a professional nurse is a strong indication of marriage or a committed relationship to come.

Nuts To dream of nuts is lucky—unless they are damaged in any way, as this is a warning that there is deception around you. If you are cracking nuts, this signifies success in your current undertakings. Eating nuts denotes that you can look forward to improvement in your health.

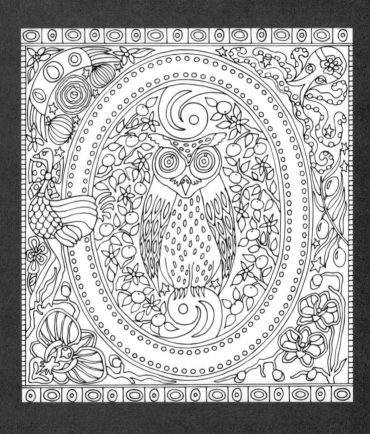

Oar   If you see yourself losing or breaking an oar, there will be problems ahead, but you will be able to overcome these problems fairly easily if you apply your logic to them.

Oasis   Dreaming of an oasis is a sign that you will achieve great success in a thrilling new adventure.

Oats   To see a crop of oats, whether in the field or harvested, foretells of financial improvement that is on the way. If the oats are unripe, this indicates that you may encounter a few problems beforehand but that these problems will not last too long. Eating oats means that steady progress will be made.

Ocean   The interpretation of this dream depends on how you see the water. If the water is calm, you can look forward to good luck. If it is rough or stormy, you will be faced with great challenges and you will need to be courageous. If the water is a little choppy, wait for some mixed luck to come to you. If you see your-self swimming in the ocean, things will soon be on the increase. An ocean voyage is an omen that you will find an answer to a frustrating problem.

Office   Dreaming of an office actually relates to emotional matters rather than business ones. If you see yourself in your own office, there is likely to be a change in your love life. A new or strange office foretells of a significant new friendship. If you are worried by things surrounding an office, this signifies family disputes.

Officer   Dreaming of a police officer warns you not to be silly about money and to be on the alert, because a friend or relative who is involved in your finances will do something stupid that makes you uncomfortable. If the officer is of a military or naval type, this indicates that you will have protection and security.

Oil   Oil seen on clothing, striking oil, or an oil field are wonderful signs of money that is about to come your way. If you are oiling machinery, you can look forward to receiving recognition for your work. Purchasing oil indicates that your love life is about to improve. Selling oil warns you to stand your ground and not give way to others. Spilling oil shows that you will have to be diplomatic. Cooking with oil signifies that someone you are unsure about can actually be trusted.

the little book of dream symbols

Olives   Whether the olives are green or ripe, seen or just being eaten, signifies happy times. Stuffed or pitted olives, however, warn that you should empathize with others more and not be so dogmatic in your attitude.

Onions   To see onions tells of a roller-coaster time of challenges. However, to see onions being eaten indicates an unexpected increase in finances. Peeling onions warns of family difficulties, particularly if you see yourself crying. Cooking onions predicts a rift with a significant friend.

Opal   Dreaming of opal is a good omen and foretells of a time of unexpected good luck.

Opera   Being at or listening to an opera is a stern warning relating to your behavior. You are not being honest and you could suffer the repercussions if found out. This is particularly so if you see opera glasses in the dream, as you will end up having to protect your name.

Operation   If you dream of undergoing surgery, be prepared for a significant change in your lifestyle.

Seeing an operation means that unexpected news is coming.

Orange To see oranges growing or in boxes indicates a slow but steady enhancement in your circumstances. Eating or drinking orange juice means that a brief but memorable love affair is on the way. Orange blossoms predict news of a forthcoming wedding.

Orchard If the orchard in your dream is in bloom, you can look forward to good luck in all areas. If the orchard contains ripening fruit, you can look forward to achieving your deepest ambition. If the fruit is unripe, your progress will be a little slower but still successful in the end.

Orders If you have to follow orders, you are in for a time of improvement. If you are giving the orders, be prepared for some family arguments.

Orphan Dreaming of an orphan is a good indication that you can expect new possessions to come your way from an unexpected source. If you dream of an

the little book of dream symbols

orphanage, this is a strong warning to you not to be egotistical, as it may result in the loss of a cherished friend.

Osteopath Dreaming of osteopaths and osteopathy shows that you will be prone to accidents in the coming weeks.

Ostrich This peculiar bird is a sign of forthcoming good luck in all areas of your life, particularly if it kicks you!

Otter This adorable creature warns that you should be watchful of your finances because you will experience some unexpected outlays.

Oven Dreaming of a hot or warm oven denotes that you will receive rewards for your efforts. If the oven is cold, you may have cause for regret, over either a friend or a chance that has been lost, but you should look forward and remain positive in your outlook.

Owl Unfortunately, to see this night bird in your dream foretells of setbacks or disillusionment. If you scare the bird away, you can look forward to progress in your state of affairs. If the owl is in the home, family dissension will follow.

Oxen This is a wonderful dream to have, as it foretells of immense success in financial matters, particularly if you see a herd of oxen grazing.

Oyster If you are opening the oysters, you are being deceived by someone you trust and you should look again before becoming involved in anything that entails friends. If you are eating oysters, you can look forward to an exciting love affair. However, if you are involved in business matters, then you need to become more forceful and active if you want to accomplish something.

Pack   Dreams of packing show that you are in a rut, and while you work hard, you are not getting anywhere.

Package   To see yourself carrying a package shows that you feel burdened by a job that you feel someone else should be doing. Speak out about it instead of keeping quiet.

Pain   The meaning varies according to the part of the body that is involved:

◊   Pain all over indicates success in your life.

◊   Pain in a limb warns that you should curb your impetuosity, as it will lead to embarrassment.

◊   Pain in the heart foretells difficulties in your love life.

◊   If the pain is felt in the chest, you can look forward to your money increasing.

◊   If the pain is felt in the head, a nasty revelation is on its way.

the little book of dream symbols

◊ If the pain is felt in the teeth, you can expect a period of trivial worries.

Paint   Painting a picture signifies that you want to keep something secret, but if you dream of painting a house, news that has been hidden from you will be revealed.

Palace   Seeing a palace from the outside signifies an improvement in your affairs. If you are inside the palace, then it is a warning not to allow your ego to get the better of you.

Palm Tree   Seeing a palm tree is a sign that someone you trust is about to let you down.

Pansies   These delightful flowers do not actually bring good news. To see them foretells that you will be on the receiving end of spite from someone of your own sex.

Parachute   If the parachute opens without any problem, then you can look forward to a contented love life. If difficulties are experienced, expect to be disappointed by someone you could normally rely upon.

Parade   To see yourself marching in a parade foretells that you will be irritated by some unexpected visitors. If you are watching a parade from the sidelines, you can look forward to an increase in your finances. If you are leading the parade, you will receive appreciation from your community.

Parcel   Receiving or mailing a parcel is an indication that you will shortly have a change in your circumstances.

Parents   Various options are:

◊   If you see your mother, you will have happiness in affairs of the heart.

◊   If you see your father, you will experience improvement in your professional life.

◊   If the parent you see is dead, some important news is coming your way.

◊   If you see other people's parents, you will receive help when you need it.

the little book of dream symbols

◊ If you see yourself as a parent, you can look forward to a surprising turnaround in something that you had given up on.

◊ If you see your parents-in-law, you must be very diplomatic in a tricky situation.

Parking   Parking a car denotes that it is time to wind down a relationship in which you have lost interest.

Party   Attending a party suggests parties and fun to come, while giving a party is an indication that disagreements lie ahead.

Path   If the path is nice and wide, you can look forward to a happy life and pleasant friends. If the path is narrow, this warns of potential problems and dishonesty from those close to you unless you remain alert.

Pearls   To see pearls, especially on a necklace, means that you are moving up in the world, but if the necklace breaks, you will suffer reversals before this happens. If you collect the pearls or restring the necklace, the setbacks will only be minor ones.

Pebbles Picking up pebbles denotes a time of loneliness due to a broken relationship. Tossing pebbles is a warning to curb your tongue as it could have repercussions. Walking or sitting on pebbles indicates that you will soon take revenge on someone.

Pen News from a distance is indicated when you dream of a pen. If the pen is unusable, it is a warning that you may suffer repercussions from the type of people with which you are associating.

Perfume When a woman dreams of using perfume, it signifies an unusual new love interest. For a man, this suggests problems in both his personal and business matters. To smell heavy perfume in a dream brings an ardent love affair. Lighter perfume indicates a happy but not so thrilling love affair.

Photographs Looking at photos indicates that you will renew an old friendship .

Piano If you are playing the piano, you can look forward to success, but if the piano is damaged, there will be some minor setbacks. If someone else is playing the piano, this signifies money to come.

Pin   Seeing pins in a dream points toward minor irritations. Being pricked by a pin suggests that you will have to help a friend out. Pinning articles of clothing indicates that you will be embarrassed socially.

Pineapple   This is a lucky dream that indicates success. Serving or eating a pineapple relates to your social life. Drinking the juice refers to your business matters. Growing or harvesting pineapples relates to your love life.

Plant   Seeing succulent green plants is a good sign of luck. If the plants are in a poor condition, you need to revise any plans or you may encounter difficulties. Planting, repotting, or watering plants indicates a pleasant home life.

Play   If you are watching a play, it means that you will have an enjoyable time, unless you disliked the play, which means that you must take care about money matters. If you see children playing, this is great news for your love life.

Pocket   Finding things in your pocket means that you can expect help from someone in authority.

A problem will resolve itself easily. Being aware of pockets in your dream indicates that you will be irritated by a mean-minded friend. A hole in the pocket means that you are being impulsive.

Police   This is a contrary dream, as seeing police in any situation symbolizes security and assistance from an unexpected quarter.

Pool   A full swimming pool foretells of happy occasions ahead. If the pool is empty, dirty, or damaged, it is not the time to gamble. A garden pool symbolizes that your love life will be blissful. Playing a game of pool shows that you need to find new friends and hobbies.

Portrait   Having your portrait painted means disappointment in affairs of the heart. Seeing someone else having his or her portrait painted denotes a rise in status for you. Receiving or giving a portrait shows that you are the victim of false flattery.

Potato   Planting, digging, cooking, or purchasing potatoes tells of luck in business matters. Eating potatoes means that you can look forward to a time of tranquillity and security. This can also mean that you should become more down-to-earth or that you should get down to doing the things that matter, while leaving things that are unnecessary.

Pregnancy   If you are a woman, you can look forward to a prosperous gain. If you are a man, this warns that you should not have indiscriminate sexual relationships.

Prize   This is a good dream, especially if you are receiving the prize, as it indicates success in all areas. If you are giving the prize, you can look forward to an increase in your finances.

Publicity   Dreaming of publicity is a warning that you should be more diplomatic.

Quantity   Seeing a large amount of anything means that you feel overwhelmed. Remain calm.

Quarrel   If you are quarreling with a stranger in your dream, it shows that something you consider a threat is not as bad as you think.

Quay   If you see a quay with no ships alongside, it warns of disillusionment due to lack of effort, but if there are ships alongside, you can look forward to future travel.

Questions   If you are asking questions, things are looking up, but if others are questioning you, you have some difficulties ahead.

Quicksand   If you are being sucked into quicksand, it is a warning not to become involved in other people's business. If you pull someone out, you can look forward to a slow improvement in money matters.

Quilt   This is a happy dream, as it indicates family bliss. A sumptuous quilt signals a great increase in wealth.

Quip An exciting invitation is on its way if you hear someone making an amusing quip or joke. Expect to visit new places and see new faces if you make a clever quip yourself!

Quiz The future will look bright or dim, depending on whether or not you gave the right or wrong answers on the quiz in the dream.

the little book of dream symbols

Rabbit Seeing rabbits in your dream shows that your responsibilities are about to be increased but that they will not feel burdensome.

Race If you are running in a race, you are about to receive a thrilling new offer. If you are watching a race, you can look forward to achievement.

Radio Listening to a radio at normal volume playing something you like means that you will have a happy family life. If the radio is too loud or annoys you in some way, you will need to resolve disagreements.

Raft To see yourself floating on a raft signifies that your laziness will lead to someone else taking advantage of you. Building or maintaining a raft is a sign that you will prosper through your own efforts.

Rage Dreaming of being in a rage means that you need to curb your temper or you are in danger of losing the support of a significant friend. If you are attempting to curb someone's rage, this warns that your current plans are not sound.

Rain The translation of a dream about rain is dependent upon the type of rain:

◊ Soft rain signifies that you are about to reap the benefits of past efforts.

◊ Drizzly rain means you will have minor obstacles to overcome, but they will disappear quickly.

◊ Light rain shows that you can look forward to a successful outcome of an affair that is not going too well.

◊ Heavy rain indicates a significant improvement, unless you are rich, in which case it means the opposite.

◊ If you are soaked in a storm, you can look forward to an unanticipated legacy.

Rainbow Seeing a rainbow is very lucky, as it means that your troubles will vanish and great happiness will follow.

Rat   These horrible rodents show that jealousy is around you.

Rattlesnake   Unsurprisingly, a rattlesnake is a sign that you have a friend around you in whom you have misplaced your trust. If the snake bites you, you are in for a difficult time, and you need to fight back.

Razor   To dream of cutting yourself on a razor or blade signifies that you will have to overcome hostilities before you can achieve what you are aiming for.

Relatives   If you dream of an aunt or uncle, financial gain will be yours. To dream of cousins indicates that your worries will soon be over. Dreaming of other family members, apart from your immediate family, foretells that you will receive help when you need it.

Rescue   If you are the one being rescued, prepare for a period of being accident-prone. If you or others are doing the rescuing, you will unexpectedly triumph over a previous problem.

Resignation   This is a contrary dream because it means that you can look forward to slow progression.

the little book of dream symbols

Restaurant   Money matters are not good, and the better the restaurant, the worse the problem. However, business will lead to socializing.

Rice   If you are picking rice or seeing it harvested, your business affairs are on the up and up. If you are cooking the rice, some difficulties you have been experiencing will have to be resolved. To eat rice is an extremely lucky omen of domestic bliss.

Ring   Receiving or giving a ring symbolizes a new love interest on the horizon. Losing or breaking a ring brings luck in business affairs.

River   If you are sitting or walking along a riverbank, continued success will be yours. If you fall into a river, some family arguments are likely. If you jump into a river, it is a warning that you should not be too hasty in your decisions.

Road   If the road is wide and in a good state of repair, you can look forward to a slow but successful progression. If the road is poor and narrow, you will have challenges to meet. To see road signs is an indication that there will be small but satisfying changes in your lifestyle.

Robber　To see a robber is a warning that, unless you are careful, you are about to let your heart rule your head over someone who is not what he or she seems.

Rock　As expected, this presents an obstacle, and you will have to be patient if you wish to triumph over difficulties. If you succeed in moving the rock or climbing over it, you will see gradual development in all matters. A rock fall suggests that a change is about to take place.

Roof　The meaning is dependent upon the type of roof:

◊　A tiled roof indicates that success is coming quickly.

◊　A shingle roof is an indication that you are lacking security emotionally.

◊　A thatched roof warns of threat through gossiping.

◊ To fall from a roof signifies a quick and satisfying short-lived success.

◊ To see a roof on fire means you are worrying needlessly.

Room Rooms, houses, kitchens, attics, and cellars relate to your state of mind, so the condition of these places shows how things are for you now and what you fear.

Rope A coil of rope indicates a solution to a problem, but if you are uncoiling the rope, you are about to start of fresh phase in your life.

Roses If you are giving roses, love will be yours. If you are receiving the roses, you can look forward to astonishing social accomplishment. If you are collecting fresh roses, happiness is assured. Artificial roses warn you that there is a dishonest friend around.

Rugby Playing rugby means that a financial gain is coming to you. Watching rugby warns that you must be choosier about your friends.

Ruins   Ancient ruins seen in your dream are a lucky sign that your circumstances are about to change for the better. A new building that is ruined signifies that sad news is on the way concerning someone close to you.

Running   You feel like running away from your present life; if you are unable to run, this suggests that you need to be more self-assertive.

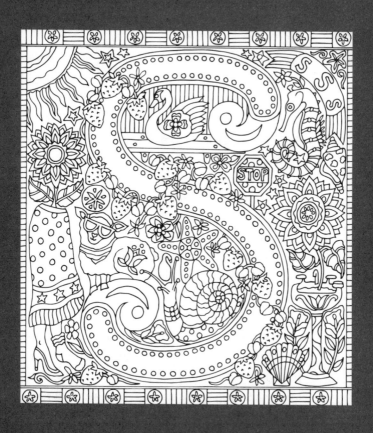

Sack Something unexpected is on the way.

Saddle This represents an enjoyable and profitable trip.

Sadness This is a contrary dream, as being aware of feeling this emotion means that your problems will soon be over.

Safe If the safe in the dream is full, you will experience a period of unforeseen problems. However, if the safe is empty, you will ultimately be successful no matter how many difficulties you encounter.

Safety Pin This is a very lucky dream. You can look forward to achievement by continuing what you are already doing.

Sailing If you are sailing in good weather and wind, affluence will be yours, but you will become disillusioned if the sea is rough. If you are coming into harbor in a small craft, unexpected success or wealth is forecast. Seeing or handling sails is a sign that happiness is at hand.

Sailor If you dream you are a sailor, you need a change of scenery. If you see sailors ashore, you can look forward to an electrifying new love interest. A solution to an outstanding financial matter is predicted when you see sailors on board ship.

Salad Eating or serving a salad predicts forthcoming luck. For a woman to dream that she is preparing a salad, this warns against being too flirtatious. For a man to have this dream, this warns that his love is misplaced.

Salmon Travel is on your personal agenda, as this suggests that you will see something of the world before settling down.

Salt Salt is said to keep the devil or evil influences away, and it is a symbol of protection. You obviously need some kind of protection, so this dream is warning you to take steps to protect yourself and your home.

Sandals Seeing or wearing a comfortable pair of sandals signifies a new love affair.

Sapphire If you are wearing this beautiful jewel, you are being too impulsive, but seeing the gem on others signifies that you will rise in status through the help of powerful associates.

Sardines If you have a new lover or if you find one soon, be sure he or she is right for you.

Satan Dreaming of the devil is a warning against bad behavior.

Saucepan Battles are ahead.

Sausages Sausages represent unexpected luck in financial or business affairs. Eating them is a warning that you could become embroiled in a love triangle.

Saw You will be busy and full of energy. Your home life will be full and happy. A rusty saw warns against accidents but any kind of saw is a good omen as far as money is concerned.

Scar To see a scar or scars on yourself is a warning that you should not do what you are contemplating.

If the scar is seen on others, you are in for a roller-coaster ride for a while.

School   Seeing yourself in school signifies that it is now time to let the past go.

Scissors   Seeing scissors is an indication that a relationship is about to break up. Using the scissors suggests that you could overcome the outcome if you act quickly.

Scorpion   A Scorpio person may enter your life soon and be a good influence on you. However, this dream also warns about treachery and friends who turn on you, unless you kill the scorpion in your dream, in which case, you overcome your enemies.

Scythe   This suggests that you should cut off from someone who is a pain in the neck. It can indicate problems in your love life.

Searching   You are knocking yourself out for others and your efforts are a waste of time.

Seat   If you fall off a seat, you can expect to lose your job. If the seat is a comfortable armchair, you are simply being shown that you need a rest.

Seeds   This is a powerful dream that shows you sowing the seeds that will create your future.

Sewing   If you are the one who is sewing, you can look forward to a surprising but thrilling new opportunity coming; if others are sewing, change your plans.

Sex   Often sexy dreams are the body's way of checking that everything is in working order. If you find yourself dreaming of sex fairly regularly, this is your subconscious telling you that it is time that you found a loving partner. If your dreams are kinky, don't worry, this is just your mind's way of experimenting with things that you would never wish to do in real life.

Shadow   Being aware of your own shadow relates to legal matters that bring an unexpected gain, but if the shadow is someone else's, this warns that you should not travel for a few weeks.

Shaking Hands   You will receive help from influential people.

Shark   As expected, this is a warning dream that relates to untrustworthy friends or business colleagues; you should be extremely careful in all money matters.

Shells   Nutshells signify success, providing they are full. If they are empty, frustration is ahead. Seashells indicate that you are in for surprises. Listening to a seashell suggests unusual news coming from afar.

Ship   Any type of ship foretells of luck in business matters. To be shipwrecked is an indication that you will have to defend yourself.

Shirt   Dreaming of a shirt means that you will be unfaithful to your lover and then split up. Wearing a dirty shirt is a warning about infection and disease. Clearly shirts are bad things to dream about!

Shoes   New and comfortable shoes indicate that you need to curb your ego. Old and worn shoes indicate success. If you lose shoes, you need to change direction; if you polish shoes, you will become involved in a surprising new venture.

Shooting Star   Great success.

Shop   A nice, clean, tidy shop is an indication of success to come, but if it is a mess, you probably have to sort something out in your own life that is a mess.

Shower   Being caught in a shower is a sign of creative success—possibly of an artistic or musical kind. If you take a shower, it is because you feel the need to get something or somebody out of your life.

Silver   Silver money in a dream signifies that your finances will be plentiful but not without the burdens that come with it. Silverware of any type suggests that you should not be so materialistic but should look inward more.

Sister   For a woman to dream of her sister predicts forthcoming family arguments. For a man to have this dream, he can look forward to being emotionally secure.

the little book of dream symbols

Skating If you are roller- or ice-skating, good times are ahead. If you fall or drop through the ice, this warns against using others to get what you want.

Skidding Dreaming of skidding denotes that you are being indecisive, but if you regain control from the skid, your finances are about to take an upturn.

Skin Beautiful and smooth skin is an indication of a contented love life. Blemished skin signifies that you need to look at your love life and make it less complicated. Peeling skin foretells of an unsatisfactory period but suggests that a blissful new relationship will soon follow.

Slip Dreaming of slipping is a warning that you should be careful in whom you place your trust.

Smoke Seeing smoke and knowing where it comes from foretells an improvement in your finances. If the source is unknown or if you smell it, you are in for a period of minor frustrations.

Snake Snakes in a dream warn of forthcoming problems and deceit.

Soccer   Playing soccer means that a financial gain is coming to you. Watching soccer warns that you must be choosier about your friends.

Soldiers   For a woman to see soldiers in a dream is a warning not to enter into casual love affairs. For a man, this means he can look forward to unexpected changes in his business affairs.

Spend   Any form of spending in a dream is a warning that you need to cut back and guard your finances.

Spider   It is very lucky for you to dream of spiders. If you kill one, good news is on its way. To see one spinning a web is a sign of money coming to you. If it is climbing a wall, success in all that you do is assured.

Spire   To see a spire indicates that true love and friendships are yours. However, you have problems to overcome if the spire is leaning or twisted.

Spy   If you are the spy, a thrilling new escapade will come your way. If you are being spied on, it is time to curb your behavior.

Stairs   Generally, up is good and down is bad. However, if you fall downstairs, you need to be less outspoken. Falling upstairs indicates a happy love life. Sweeping stairs means that you can look forward to a surprising upturn in your lifestyle.

Stamps   Purchasing stamps signifies material gains. Placing stamps on a letter foretells that your position is about to improve.

Stars   Bright and twinkling stars predict that you will achieve success through the help of a significant friend of the opposite sex. Many stars predict success. A shooting star indicates that you will succeed, but not quite as quickly as you want.

Steal   Stealing in a dream is a warning that you should be extremely careful with all money matters over the following months. If you are caught, good luck is assured.

Stones   If you are throwing stones, you regret missing an opportunity. Stepping-stones indicate improvement, albeit slowly. Cobblestones warn against gambling.

S

Storms Dreaming of storms is a strong indication of a time of forthcoming problems and reminds you that you are the only one who can change things for yourself.

Strangling If you are strangled or are being strangled, you need to free yourself from your own fears. If you are doing the strangling, follow your intuition in relation to someone you do not entirely trust.

Straw Stacks of straw are a good indication of financial gains. Wet straw tells that bad behavior could be your undoing. Burning straw signifies that you must guard against carelessness with your finances, while dreaming of sleeping on straw means that you will fight with a lover.

Stream A clear stream that flows smoothly is a sign of the way that your own life is flowing. A rough or murky stream means that things are not good right now.

Street To see a very long street is an indication that you will have to be patient before you can achieve

the little book of dream symbols

what you want. A strange street foretells of success through new contacts. Crooked or curving streets predict travel and revelations.

Sun A bright, sunny day predicts success. An overcast sun is a warning of family disputes. A red sun denotes struggle but suggests that you will triumph in the end. New doors are about to open for you if you see a sunrise. A setting sun foretells of a thrilling change for the better.

Surf To see surf breaking is an indication that a small but good change in your love life or business matters is in the cards.

Swamp Walking in a swamp is a severe warning that it is time to break off a relationship that has become dangerous to you. Being lost in a swamp warns that you need to take greater control of your finances.

Swim If you are swimming in a pool, this warns of hidden resentment around you. If you are swimming toward the shore, you will have financial security, but only through your own hard work. Swimming in a costume means that you are in for an embarrassing time, but if you are naked, you will have good luck in all that you do. Watching others swimming predicts good luck.

the little book of dream symbols

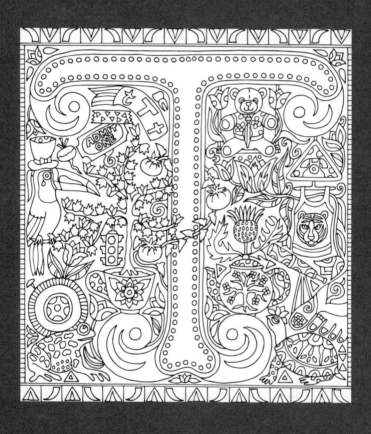

Table The significance of a table depends upon its condition. An isolated table speaks of a peaceful future, while one that is loaded down with food talks of happy gatherings. A dirty or broken table signifies family arguments.

Tacks Sharp nails or tacks warn of irritations and possibly of being on the end of someone else's sarcastic or hurtful remarks.

Tailor Dreaming of a tailor warns you to avoid putting yourself in a position where others can criticize you or where their plans can hurt you. A woman who dreams of a tailor might marry beneath her. Otherwise, this means wasted journeys, wasted time, and misunderstandings.

Talking You are having a hard time getting your points across to others. If you hear others talking, this can mean that your spiritual guides are close by and that they will help you.

Tambourine This is an indication of festivities, celebrations, and fun.

Tap (Faucet)   This shows that money and other good things will soon be coming your way.

Tarot   If you see a specific card in your dream, you need to research the tarot to see what the card means. A deck of cards suggests that you could do with a reading yourself or that you may wish to take up tarot reading yourself.

Tassel   Dreaming of ropes or fringes that end in a tassel suggests that you will soon bring a situation to an end, and everybody who is involved will be pleased with the outcome.

Taxi   If you dream of a taxi during the daytime, this is good news for your career, as it seems to be on the way up. If it is at night, there is a warning that you should keep secrets.

Taxman   It is not unusual for people to dream of tax inspectors, accountants, and such, and it is usually a warning to keep an eye on finances and to pay those to whom you are in debt. It can also mean that you will be faced with an unexpected large household bill.

Tea   You can expect friendship and some free time in which to sit around and gossip harmlessly with your pals. If you see a teapot that is dirty or broken, you can expect gossip and scandal.

Teeth   Dreaming of teeth is amazingly common, and practical reasons may be that you grind your teeth in your sleep or that you need to visit a dentist. If you suffer from headaches or migraine, it might be worth looking into this, because tooth grinding can bring this on. On the other hand, this can indicate the loss of a friend or relative or sickness in the family. Some traditions suggest that this is a good omen about money, but the teeth would have to be in excellent condition for that to be the case.

Telephone   Telephones, telegrams, and emails all foretell interesting news.

Temptation   You may dream about a delicious cake, a drink that you shouldn't have or some kind of sexual indiscretion. That's fine—as long as the dream doesn't become reality.

Tent   A long period of instability is on the way to you especially regarding your home and your domestic arrangements. You may change houses or travel a lot in the near future, and you can't look forward to a settled situation for some time to come.

Theater   Be careful what you say and to whom you say it. If the theater is empty, you are in for some form of heartache.

Thief, Theft   This is a straightforward warning that might indicate a robbery, or that you are being ripped off in some way.

Thorn   A thorn pricking you in the head signifies grief; it signifies pain and loss if it is in your arm or hand, and a change of address if it is in your foot.

Throat   This is a factual dream that warns of a sore throat or a cold to come.

Throne   If the throne is broken or empty, there may be some kind of downfall in your family circle.

Thunder Don't upset those who have authority over you or those who have the power to make your life difficult.

Tie If you were wearing a tie in your dream or if you helped a man to put on one, this represents a forthcoming formal event or formal occasion.

Tiger This is a clear warning of danger—particularly of hidden danger. Oddly enough, it can be a warning that someone around you is taking drugs!

Tobacco This is not a good sign if you are in business or are buying or selling something important. It could all go up in smoke.

Toboggan Sometimes events come along that we cannot control and this is what this dream is telling you. You may be sliding into some kind of trouble and while it will take courage to stop the rot, you will have to do so.

Tomato Success is on the way to you if you are growing tomatoes in your dream. Socializing and good times are on the way if you are eating them.

the little book of dream symbols

These are sometimes associated with enjoyable times that are filled with love and sex.

Tomb Dreams of graves, tombs, and so on are usually an indication of a fresh start. Perhaps it is time to bury the past and move on. Some old traditions suggest that you might start to research your family tree. You feel trapped by the past and your thinking is being influenced by the opinions of people who are no longer part of your life and who are no longer relevant to you.

Tongs This indicates restlessness and dissatisfaction. You may go through a period of sleeplessness soon due to worry.

Torch (Flashlight) You are desperate for change and to see a clearer future ahead. You may part from your lover soon.

Torture Whether you are torturing others or being tortured, the dream is telling you to go easy on yourself and not to put yourself through unnecessary stress.

Tower If the tower is intact, your life is improving. If it is broken, beware of trouble to come.

Train Any dream of movement indicates important journeys, but this can also suggest that you will struggle with a problem until you overcome it. Friends might let you down. If the train is the kind that we used to see on a wedding dress, and if you are a woman who is hoping that a man will commit himself to you, it won't happen.

Trap The meaning of this dream is obvious. Something that you are being asked to do or something that you are contemplating going into is a trap. You know it—at least your sleeping, subconscious self knows it—so now you have to understand this consciously and take appropriate action.

Travel Travel dreams are extremely common, and it is easy to work out their meaning. For example, if you are traveling happily in your dream, you can be sure that your pathway through life will be smooth. If your journey is obstructed, uncomfortable, delayed, and so on, or if you lose your luggage along the way, there is interference in your life or too many obstacles for you to cope with at present.

Treasure   If you find treasure in your dream, your finances are set to improve, but if you lose it, you can expect losses.

Trees   Symbolically, trees are a symbol of growth, abundance, prosperity, hope, love, and good fortune, but it depends upon the condition of the tree. In a poor condition, the tree is warning you to look for some other means of earning money. If you cut a tree down, you can expect some really heavy losses, but it may be for the best in that you need to clear the way for something new to come into your life.

Trial   Dreaming of being on trial shows that you will have to answer for your actions. If you were conducting the trial, this means that you will soon have to dig around to discover the true facts of a situation.

Triangle   This signifies talent and creativity that you will soon tap into and create success out of.

Triumph Dreams of victory and triumph suggest that you will overcome a problem soon.

Trolley Whether this is a supermarket trolley or some other kind of trolley, the meaning is that you will have to push hard to make something come right in your life. It won't happen of its own accord, so it will be up to you to make the effort to bring about the desired result.

Trombone There are two meanings to this dream. The first is that you may meet someone who you fall in love with but who in the long run is not right for you. The second is that you may march, hike, or otherwise find yourself traveling on foot.

Trumpet There will soon be an announcement about something good.

Trunk Pack your bags, you are going on a trip and it might change your life.

Turquoise This stone brings peace and calm to a troubled mind, so perhaps you ought to consider wearing some for a while.

Tusk This is a lucky dream as it signifies better times, especially regarding love and sex.

Twins You may find that you have more on your plate than you can cope with for a while. This can be an indication that a Gemini person will soon be important to you or that something will happen during the late spring.

Ugliness   It is an unlucky omen to see an ugly person. If you are the one who looks ugly in the dream, you need to be more outgoing in order to maintain your friendships.

Umbrella   If the umbrella is furled, you can expect a bit of peace; otherwise be prepared for others to blame you unjustly or to misunderstand your motives. Friends might cost you money.

Undressing   Dreaming of being naked or undressing in inappropriate circumstances is a warning to be discreet. Otherwise, it may mean that you are fed up with having to put on an act for the benefit of others or fed up with not being yourself.

Unfaithfulness   Everybody dreams of being unfaithful to their partner at times, however much they love each other. This is nature's way of allowing you to experiment in safety. Don't worry about it.

Unhappy   This is a contrary dream. The more unhappy you feel, the happier you will become.

Uniform   Influential friends will come to your aid. If you dream of a uniform, it can also indicate love and passion.

Urination   This is a common dream, and it usually means that you need to use the bathroom. Hopefully, you will wake up and relieve the pressure . . .

University   This is an especially promising dream for those attending a university. If you are not at college, you can look forward to success in business or politics.

Urn   Strangely enough, dreaming of an urn symbolizes prosperity.

the little book of dream symbols

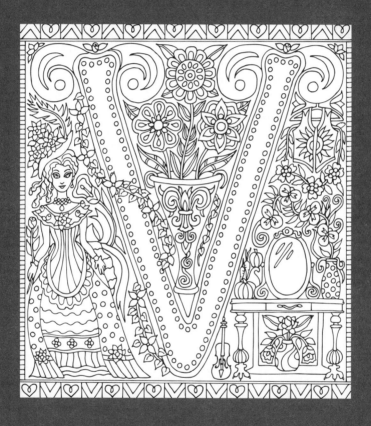

Valentine Dreaming of receiving a valentine card or gift indicates that a gift, money, or a pleasant surprise is on the way to you. In other circumstances, an old flame may contact you. If you send a valentine in your dream, you are probably throwing your love away on a reluctant lover.

Valley This is a good dream as far as business is concerned, unless the valley is muddy or flooded, in which case it can symbolize restriction and sickness.

Vampire Common sense will tell you that someone is taking advantage of you, and your lover might be a parasite who makes use of you. If you see this dream more than once, it can predict a death somewhere around you.

Vegetable Vegetable dreams foretell hard work and the need to persist. This can also signify that you need to focus on what is important and get rid of the things that are unimportant.

Vehicle Dreams of vehicles are surprisingly common. If you are buying one, you can expect things to look up, but if you are selling one, you may be in for trouble at work. Riding in one can denote sickness or loss, while being thrown from one indicates failure.

Veil   The color of the veil is significant, because if it is white, it refers to a probable marriage, but if it is black, it predicts a time of mourning. Gray symbolizes a useful life, and pink may relate to false modesty, while blue demands that you take precautions of some kind.

Vengeance   This is a practical dream that shows you taking revenge on someone who has hurt you.

Verandah   The condition of the verandah is important, as a nice one denotes family happiness and love, while a decrepit one signals the opposite.

Vermin   This is a common dream; it denotes petty irritations.

Vicar   This might indicate a wedding, baptism, or something similar, but it can also signify reconciliation.

Vise Dreaming of a vise warns against getting into the grip of something that is hard to get out of.

Vines, Vineyard Abundance, luck, and plenty will come your way.

Violets Violets are a symbol of true love and real affection and spiritual development.

Virgin This is a lovely dream if you are a Christian because it indicates that the Virgin will help you to recover and to feel better about things. Otherwise, it can indicate taking on something completely new.

Visits, Visiting, Visitors If you like visitors, this is a nice dream to have, but if you are looking for some peace and quiet, this suggests that you will not have any for a while. Take note of whether your visits or visitors pleased you or not. If you dream that a doctor pays you a visit (an unlikely event in real life), it is a warning about your health.

Votes Voting or electing signifies that you will soon have to rely upon others.

Vulture Needless to say, this is not a good omen. People might take advantage of you or you may have a serious opponent to deal with. Old-time dream interpreters saw this as an omen of famine!

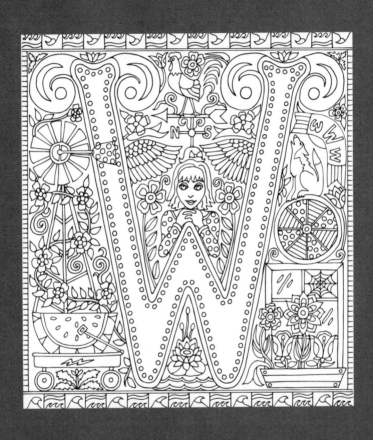

Wading This dream is great for you and your lover if the water is clear, but if it is muddy, the affair will not go well. If you are walking against the flow, the relationship is going nowhere.

Walking A pleasant walk in the countryside denotes that your life will be easy, but if you walk through mud, briars, or unpleasant places, it means that people around you will be difficult. A very long walk indicates difficulties at work, while a swaggering walk suggests that you are being too proud or arrogant. A very old tradition says that if you walk under a horse and a sparrow's nest falls on you and scatters dirt on your face, you can expect an attack of shingles!

Walls Any dream that involves walls tells you that you have obstacles to overcome or that the walls are closing in on you.

War You will soon have a fight on your hands. Check whether you win or lose the war in your dream.

Warehouse An empty warehouse symbolizes a shortage of the things you need, while a full one shows an abundance of goodies.

Washing   This is indicative of a desire to lead a better life, but it can also mean defending a friend who is under attack.

Water   The meaning of the dream depends upon the condition of the water:

◊   Clean water signifies prosperity, happiness, and a successful journey.

◊   Muddy or dirty water suggests unhappiness.

◊   If you see water coming into your house, do not be too trusting.

◊   Playing with water indicates passion, while having it sprayed on your head is an even stronger indication of love and passion.

◊   If you are playing among waves, this shows problems in your love life, unless the waves subside in your dream, in which case troubles will soon iron themselves out.

Wedding   Usually this is a contrary dream that predicts sad news, loss of love, or family problems, but if you are holding a bouquet at the wedding, it predicts that you will soon be a bridesmaid. A wedding cake indicates prosperity and a happy marriage.

Weeds   Weeds in your garden indicate that you have too much work to cope with. If you are burning weeds, this indicates that you are dodging your responsibilities.

Wheel   If the wheel is turning, you can expect a change for the better, but if it is still, you must expect delays to your plans. If the wheel is broken, an inheritance that should come your way will be taken by others or squandered by them. If the wheel is moving uphill, life may be hard, but you will achieve your aims; if it is rolling downhill and runs out of control, your life is also running downhill and out of control.

Whip   If you are about to enter into a marriage or commitment, stop and think, because it may turn out to be extremely unpleasant.

Will   Dreaming of making your will shows that other people will try to take advantage of you, and losing a will shows a poor outlook for business or health.

Wind If a strong wind blows, you can expect opposition, but if the breeze is gentle, things will go smoothly.

Windmill If the windmill is moving, things will be unsettled for a while, but if the sun shines on it, you can expect success.

Window If the window is open, your problems will be solved; if it is closed, there may be unexpected danger, although you will be saved from real harm.

Witch This predicts difficulties in the home and for members of your family, but good news for travelers. If you dream that a witch has put a spell on you, take care that you don't fall under a bad influence.

Wolf If you dream of a wolf, you may suffer business losses due to theft or people taking advantage of you; this can also mean unpleasant neighbors.

Wood If you hide in a wood, this shows that you feel unhappy about your own behavior.

Worms   Worm dreams are extremely common; they show that you are worried and anxious.

Wound   Dreaming of being hurt shows that someone may attack your character.

Wrestling   You will have to fight hard for something that you want to have or to achieve, but you will triumph in the end.

Writing   Something is wrong and you must put it right.

X Known as *Gifu* or *Gyfu* in the Runes, an X means that a time of giving and receiving is on the way—you can expect a gift to come to you. Remember: gifts can be emotional rather than material!

X-mas As expected, dreaming of Christmas denotes a time of celebrations and happiness coming your way. Expect family reunions and festivities.

X-ray Changes are going on behind the scenes, but these changes should suit you.

Xerox Dreaming of photocopies or photocopiers means that you are in danger of repeating past mistakes. It is time to put things in order.

Xylophone You may be asked to participate in a pageant. If you hear a xylophone being played and it is out of tune, beware of forthcoming accidents.

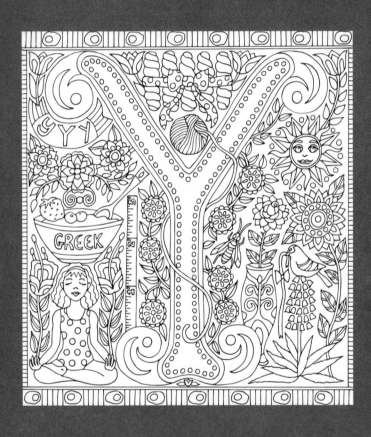

Yacht Life will be changeable and risky.

Yarn Yarn, as in knitting or other kinds of yarn, implies a long, happy, and productive life. An old interpretation is that a woman will marry someone who is down the social ladder from her, but that he will turn out to be an excellent husband.

Yawn This dream shows that you are so fed up with your life as it is at the moment that you may walk out and even travel to other countries for a while.

Yell Hearing yourself yell in a dream is a warning that you are about to be discovered in underhanded dealings. A friend will be asking for your help if the yell comes from someone else.

Yew Tree Dreaming of a yew tree is a generally good omen other than if you have older relatives, as this can predict that one is nearing the end of life.

Yoke You will have to fall in with other people's plans. If you marry soon, you will be happy with your partner.

Yolk   One old tradition says that if you dream of the yolk of an egg, you will win the lottery. If there ever was a case for directed or lucid dreaming, this is it!

Yucca   Dreaming of this succulent and beautiful desert plant is a promise of both spiritual and material comforts in life.

Zebra Dreaming of a zebra suggests a disagreement or cross-purposes.

Zipper Your dignity will be maintained despite enormous provocation if you are fastening your own zipper. However, if the zipper gets stuck, you will suffer unpleasant consequences through the actions of one of your friends.

Zircon This stone is known as "The Prudent One," and it means that you have misplaced your emotions. You need to examine your close relationships and be less trusting with others.

Zodiac There are many strange meanings to this one. For example, it is said to foretell dreadful storms. On the face of things, that is a ridiculous thing to dream about, but in these days of global warming it is not that strange. Other interpretations suggest travel, others thinking well of you, improved finances, and fame.

Zoo A number of options are opening up to you, including happy marriage, travel, and success.

About the Author

When Jacqueline Towers was fourteen, she had a terrifying out-of-body event and subsequently experienced a number of other inexplicable events. Interested in learning more about the psychic world after her experiences, she taught herself to read playing cards.

As is often the way with professional psychics, a series of immense difficulties placed Jackie on her psychic path. As a single mother with two young children and little money, Jackie worked as a legal secretary during the day and studied the tarot during the evenings. She eventually became a Reader and started to give tarot readings on a semi-professional basis.

Gordon Arthur Smith, the late well-known British Astrological and Psychic Society medium and healer, guided Jackie in her career as a medium, psychometrist, and qualified Reiki healer.

Jackie currently gives demonstrations at Spiritualist churches, lectures at workshops on psychic subjects, and is the vice-chairman of the British Astrological and Psychic Society (BAPS). She is also an editor and designer for the BAPS magazine.